COMBAT LEGEND

F-16
FIGHTING
FALCON

Kev Darling

Airlife

Copyright © 2003 Airlife Publishing Ltd

Text written by Kev Darling
Profile illustrations created by Dave Windle
Cover painting by Jim Brown – The Art of Aviation Co. Ltd

First published in the UK in 2003
by Airlife Publishing Ltd

British Library Cataloguing-in-Publication Data
A catalogue record for this book
is available from the British Library

ISBN 1 84037 399 7

Printed in China

*Contact us for a free catalogue that describes the complete range of Airlife
books for pilots and aviation enthusiasts*

Airlife Publishing Ltd
101 Longden Road, Shrewsbury, SY3 9EB, England
E-mail: sales@airlifebooks.com
Website: www.airlifebooks.com

Contents

F-16 Timeline

2 February 1974
Maiden flight of first YF-16.

January 1975
The USAF selects the F-16 as its air combat fighter and announces plans to procure at least 650. Belgium, Denmark, Norway, and the Netherlands announce plans to buy 348 F-16s on 7 June.

February 1978
First European F-16 assembly line opens in Belgium.

April 1978
Second European assembly line opens in the Netherlands.

6 January 1979
Delivery of first operational F-16 to USAF's 388th Tactical Fighter Wing, Hill AFB, Utah.

26 January 1979
Belgian Air Force accepts first European-assembled F-16.

June 1981
First F-16 combat use, in Israel's raid on an Iraqi nuclear reactor.

July 1984
First F-16C is delivered to USAF.

June 1987
First Block 32 F-16C/Ds delivered to USAF.

December 1988
First Block 40 F-16 delivered.

January 1991
USAF F-16s enter combat in Operation *Desert Storm*.

May 1991
Belgium, Denmark, the Netherlands, and Norway affirm their commitment to the European F-16A/B Mid-Life Update (MLU) programme.

December 1992
Lockheed becomes Lockheed Martin.

December 1992
A USAF F-16C shoots down an Iraqi MiG in a no-fly zone, marking first combat kill for AMRAAM and first air-to-air combat for a US F-16.

March 1993
Lockheed Martin buys General Dynamics' military aircraft business.

May 1993
Lockheed Martin delivers first Block 50 F-16C.

4 December 1996
F-16 fleet achieves 5 million flight hours worldwide.

Mid-1998
USAF designates Block 50/52 aircraft as F-16CJ machines and dedicates them to the SEAD role. Block 40/42 aircraft become F-16CG warplanes, dedicated to ground attack using the LANTIRN system.

September 1998
Lockheed Martin awarded contract to implement Common Configuration Implementation Program for all extant F-16C/D Blocks 40/42 and 50/52 to bring them up to the same standard as European MLU. Some 700 aircraft involved.

26 March 1999
3,035th production aircraft delivered from Lockheed Martin's Fort Worth plant to the USAF.

24 March–20 June 1999
Operation *Allied Force* begins against Serbia.

March 2000
4,000th F-16 delivered.

5 March 2000
Block 60 Desert Falcon version ordered for UAE.

7 October 2001
Operation *Enduring Freedom* against the Taliban in Afghanistan begins and Operation *Noble Eagle* activated to defend the USA.

28 December 2001
Chile announces order for F-16C/D Block 52.

October 2002
USAF and allies on standby to recommence operations over Iraq.

1. Prototypes and Development

Viper to its crews, but officially Fighting Falcon, the Lockheed Martin (General Dynamics) F-16 was designed to fill a single role, but has successfully transmuted into a multi-role combat aircraft that is now in service around the globe.

In the 1950s, Lockheed's Clarence L. 'Kelly' Johnson had led development of the F-104 Starfighter, which set new standards for high performance in a lightweight airframe. However, the Starfighter was very much a product of the 1950s, where high speed and the capability to engage an enemy with air-to-air missiles (AAMs) were key qualities, not dogfighting ability. This it shared with other contemporary US fighters, but in general, aircraft such as the Convair F-102 Delta Dagger and McDonnell F-101 Voodoo were considerably heavier. This trend for complex, heavy, high-performance fighter aircraft continued into the Vietnam War, but in combat against lighter North Vietnamese MiGs, the US

Airborne on an early sortie is the first YF-16, 72-1567, which made its official maiden flight on 2 February 1974. The aircraft wore a very patriotic red, white and blue scheme. *(via USAF)*

Extensive wind tunnel testing was carried out on the F-16 design, which ran through a gamut of wing planforms, engine intake layouts and fin configurations. That shown here is the final product.
(via USAF)

fighters were frequently at a disadvantage. Some USAF planners began considering the merits of an agile, lightweight, simple dogfighter.

The F-16 programme ultimately resulted from this original concept to produce an experimental lightweight day fighter. The concept first saw the light of day in 1965, when it was proposed as a component in a two-part fighter development programme. The other aircraft in the programme was referred to as the F-X (Fighter-Experimental), and was intended to be a heavy interceptor and air superiority fighter in the 40,000-lb (18144-kg) class. Its lightweight stablemate was to be in the 25,000-lb (11340-kg) class. The heavyweight design was seen as a platform for a sophisticated multifunction radar, which would be complemented by a selection of long-range, radar-guided missiles, all being combined in an airframe with inflight refuelling capability to extend its range. In contrast, the lightweight fighter was designated as an Advanced Day Fighter (ADF), which would have a high thrust-to-weight ratio that would improve upon that of the Mikoyan-Gurevich MiG-21 'Fishbed' by at least 25 per cent.

Wearing its Paris Air Show number '53', the first YF-16 taxies out for a display in June 1975 still wearing its brightly coloured finish. Once its period of test flying was complete, the airframe was converted for use in the CCV programme. (C P Russell Smith Collection)

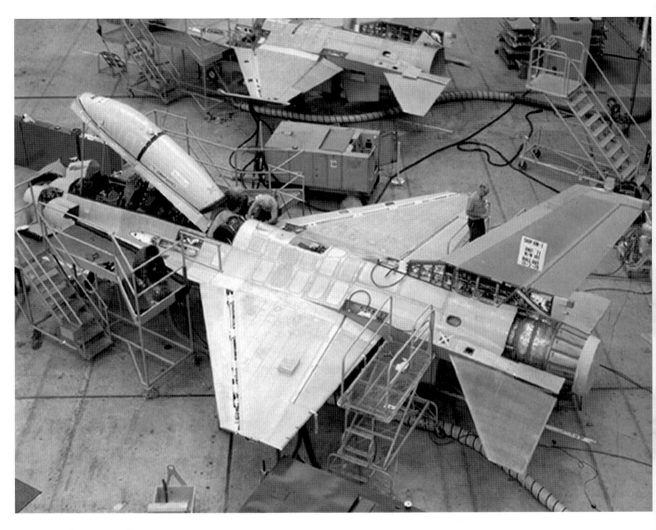

Enter the 'Foxbat'

Mikoyan-Gurevich's MiG-25 'Foxbat' came as a nasty shock to the West. This massive, twin-engined aircraft was designed as a high-speed, high-altitude interceptor. It was equipped with a sophisticated radar and long-range infra-red (IR) and radar-guided missiles. The testing of this interceptor in the Soviet Union from 1964, resulted in a reappraisal of the USAF's fighter policy. The result was a slow down of the ADF programme, while the F-X project was hugely accelerated. F-X eventually emerged as the McDonnell Douglas F-15 Eagle.

Meanwhile, some work continued on the

This two-seat F-16 was photographed on the Fort Worth construction line. *(via Lockheed Martin)*

renamed F-XX lightweight fighter concept, which had now evolved into an airframe that weighed in at 7711 kg (17,000 lb). It was to be equipped with minimal avionics and short-range missiles for the air-combat role. Understandably, with American involvement in Vietnam increasing, the USAF hierarchy was against investing precious development dollars in an aircraft that was lightly equipped and could perform just one role. in addition, it lacked all the bells and whistles that the USAF generals had come to expect. The final straw for the USAF came in 1969, when a Pentagon memorandum suggested that the F-XX replace the F-15 and the Grumman F-14 Tomcat, which was being developed for the US Navy, since the costs of both were increasing rapidly. Conscious of losing research and development dollars, as well as their heavyweight fighters, both services put up strong resistance to this move.

Lightweight Fighter project

Although the ADF project seemed to have been quashed, by 1971 it had resurfaced as the Lightweight Fighter (LWF) project. Coincidentally, it was around this time that the procurement process was changed. Gone was the total procurement package that had resulted in such aircraft as the General Dynamics F-111 fighter-bomber and the Lockheed C-5 Galaxy transport. Both had been ordered straight off the drawing board and had suffered from massive cost overruns. To replace this extravagant waste of the taxpayers' money a new proposal, called competitive prototyping, was introduced. Thus, initial funding for each project would be basic, with the resultant aircraft being built to explore the minimum parameters laid down in the development contract.

On 16 January 1971 the LWF requirement officially came into being, with the issuance of a request for proposals (RFP) to the aviation industry. The specifications laid down included

a high thrust-to-weight ratio, a maximum weight under 20,000 lb (9072 kg) and high manoeuvrability. Any requirement to intercept and chase aircraft such as the MiG-25 had been dropped, the manufacturers were being asked to create a fighter that could take on the Mikoyan-Gurevich MiG-17 'Fresco' and MiG-21 in close combat. It was also stressed that the aircraft should be as small as possible and that it had to be capable of speeds up to Mach 1.6. Its high thrust-to-weight ratio and high manoeuvrability would hopefully give the new fighter an edge over its Soviet-built opposition. The size requirement was borne of bitter experience, since the North Vietnamese MiGs encountered in Southeast Asia were not only manoeuvrable, but also very difficult to see thanks to their small size. These qualities combined to make them extremely difficult for the heavyweight McDonnell Douglas F-4 Phantom II to shoot down. This situation was exacerbated by the Phantom's optimisation for beyond-visual range (BVR) missile combat. The prevailing belief that all air-to-air engagements would be carried out BVR, had led the USAF and USN to place little emphasis on dogfighting skills. The US crews were therefore further hampered by a basic lack of flying technique, and this weakness led the US Navy to set up its Fighter Weapons School, or 'Top Gun', establishment. The USAF also took heed of the lessons learned at 'Top Gun' and some of these were incorporated into the LWF and F-X requirements.

The final paragraph of the LWF RFP stated that three further objectives must be met. The aircraft should take advantage of and help in the development of emerging technologies; every effort should be made to reduce the risk in the full scale and development phases; and the machine should be designed in such a way as to be capable of taking advantage of future systems and weapons developments.

The second FSD F-16, 75-0746, appeared in this warlike finish. Worthy of note are the engine air start and air conditioning trolley hoses plugged into the aircraft. *(Scott Van Aken)*

Festooned with AGM-65 Maverick missiles, AIM-9 Sidewinders, a LANTIRN pod and other equipment under development is FSD F-16, 75-0750, which has been converted to AFTI standard. The missile spread was fitted for use during the close air support development trials. *(Scott Van Aken)*

RFP responses

In response to the Pentagon's RFP the design teams at Boeing, General Dynamics (GD), Northrop, Ling-Temco-Vought and Lockheed were busy preparing proposals for consideration. By this time McDonnell Douglas was deeply involved in turning its F-X proposal into the F-15 Eagle and chose to concentrate only on progressing this contract. After the paper sift of the presented project files, the Air Staff announced in March 1972 that its preferred bidder would be Boeing with the Model 908-909, while the General Dynamics Model 401 and the Northrop Model P-600 were regarded as coming close to the ideal. The LTV V-1100 and the Lockheed CL-1200 Lancer, a development of the F-104, were eliminated, although the latter was continued as a private project.

Although Boeing had won the first round of the selection process, its position was reversed on 13 April 1972, when the Source Selection Authority recommended that the General Dynamics and Northrop designs be selected for further development. The result was that contracts were issued for a pair of Model 401-16B prototypes to be designated as YF-16s. These were serialled 72-1567 and -1568. Also receiving a development contract was the Northrop YF-17, of which two were ordered for competition and comparison purposes. It should be noted that the 'Y' prefix was used instead of the normal 'X' for experimental, since the aircraft were seen as developmental not experimental. The YF-16s would each be powered by a single Pratt & Whitney F100 turbofan, while the YF-17s would have pairs of General Electric YJ101 engines. The contracts for both types were presented as 'cost plus fixed fee', which covered the design, construction and testing of two prototypes and included 12 months of flight testing. Nevertheless, the USAF still saw the LWF as a proof-of-concept technology demonstrator, and regarded the F-15 as its primary fighter for production. In concert with the airframe manufacturers, the engine builders were given contracts to develop the relevant powerplants.

With development contracts in place, the actual design work on the YF-16 could begin. GD's Fort Worth plant in Texas was charged with creating the YF-16. The project directors were nominated as William C. Dietz and Lyman C. Josephs, with Harry Hillaker as the chief designer. Before any metal was cut on the new aircraft, an extensive regime of mathematical modelling and wind tunnel testing of mock-ups was undertaken. The final design was a blending of new materials and techniques, proved technologies and the results gained from the wind tunnel tests, the whole being broken down into easy to manufacture sub-assemblies. To keep costs in check each assembly was extensively costed to see if lower price conventional materials could be used in its manufacture, although more exotic materials and technologies were to be used where it would enhance the performance of the aircraft.

The choice of a single engine to power the YF-16 was the result of extensive testing using wind tunnel mock-ups simulating one or two engines. Also considered was the thrust-to-weight ratio of each set-up, plus the perceived rate of fuel consumption. Another benefit was weight reduction, the single-engined airframe was forecast at 17,050 lb (7734 kg), while the twin-engined aircraft worked out at 21,470 lb (9861 kg). With the engine layout settled, investigations began into the form that the vertical tail surfaces should take. Both single- and twin-fin arrangements were experimented with, the final choice being a single fin augmented by a pair of underfuselage finlets. Wind tunnel testing had revealed that although the twin fin arrangement would suffice throughout much of the flight envelope, a problem occurred at high angles-of-attack (AoA) where the vortices generated by the blended forward fuselage reduced stability. Also subjected to extensive testing was the location and shape of the intake. Eventually a position under the forward fuselage was settled upon, this minimising airflow disturbance to the engine at high AoA. From the outset a ventral location had been the favoured position, a similar layout to that of the Vought F-8 Crusader being the starting point, before the intake mouth was moved further back to save weight. The

final position also provided a location for the nose gear and its bay. Although there are numerous advantages to such an intake there is a downside. The closeness of the intake to the ground does render the engine vulnerable to foreign object damage (FOD) from stones and general runway debris, while there is also a potential danger to ground personnel. On the positive side the intake location reduces the problem of gun gas ingestion considerably, while FOD cannot be spun into the engine face by the nosewheel, which is positioned behind the intake lip. In order to further save weight, and to avoid the need to design complex drive mechanisms, the intake geometry was fixed.

Falcon wings

Having settled upon the fuselage design and the engine type, the design team turned its attention to the wing planform. Four different layouts were considered, these being straight, swept, variable and delta. The first to be rejected was the variable wing, since it was complex and heavy. Following soon after was the delta wing, which had trim drag penalties and performance problems in the turn, although it did have good weight characteristics and behaved well in level flight. The final choice was a moderately swept wing with a straight trailing edge. It was seen as providing the best combination of good manoeuvrability, high acceleration and the excellent lift characteristics that would ensure good altitude performance. Control of the wing's behaviour is courtesy of a dedicated computer system which controls the leading-edge variable camber manoeuvring flaps. The trailing edge of the wing provides mountings for the flaperons. To minimise the aircraft's weight, the wing and fuselage are carefully blended together so that there is no definable join between them. The leading edge of the wing root is faired into the forward fuselage by means of broad-chord blended strakes. These forebodies produce vortices which increase manoeuvrability at high AoA, by producing energy sufficient to excite the boundary layer over the inner section of the wing, delaying wing-root stalling and maintaining directional stability. The downside of this careful aerodynamic design was that the wing structure was too thin to house the main undercarriage units, which therefore had to be located in the lower fuselage. To maintain stability on the ground, the main gear units are quite widely splayed. The wing is manufactured mainly from aluminium alloy, although some areas are made from steel, titanium and composites. Steel is used in high-stress areas, while composites are used in lightly loaded areas and for antenna covers.

A computer generates signals which control the behaviour of the wing surfaces via the fly-by-wire (FBW) system. The latter also controls the all-flying tailplanes and the rudder. Control is via a side-stick controller, a radical choice at the time, while the ejection seat is tilted backwards by 30° to allow the pilot to absorb a load of 9 *g*. Topping the cockpit is a virtually uncluttered canopy offering excellent all-round vision.

Although the LWF development aircraft was specified to have minimal electronics, the designers recognised that there was a possibility that in service use, expansion would likely be required. Therefore, space was included for an improved avionics package while provision was made for an M61 cannon. Provision was also made for missile armament; initially this was the AIM-9 Sidewinder, although the possibility of carrying AIM-7 Sparrow missiles was also investigated as a later option.

High-*g* airframe

The original specification had laid down that the airframe should be capable of accepting a loading of 7.33 *g* throughout the combat envelope while carrying 80 per cent of its total fuel load. Such was the care taken during the initial design phase, that the General Dynamics team felt able to upgrade the maximum operating load to 9 *g* with full fuel. At the same time, airframe tweaks allowed the engineers to increase the fatigue life from the initial 4,000 hours to 8,000 hours. To give the YF-16 as much airborne time as possible, General Dynamics postulated that during a normal sortie the first leg of the mission, the transit to the combat area, would be undertaken using extra fuel housed in tanks under the wings. The remainder of the flight including the return leg would be undertaken using the internal fuel load. These changes, once accepted, meant that

FSD F-16 75-0752, was used as the Wild Weasel test-bed before being used for J79 engine trials. To accommodate the longer powerplant, the aircraft's rear fuselage was extended. The Navy titles were an attempt to sell this version to the US Navy for the DACT role. *(Scott Van Aken)*

Although it wears a USAF serial number and General Dynamics titling, this F-16B was the first for Belgium. In service it became FB-01. *(Scott Van Aken)*

the airframe empty weight could be reduced by a further 667 kg (1,470 lb). This in turn, reduced the gross weight by another 1361 kg (3,000 lb), which improved the acceleration by 30 per cent and the rate of turn by a further 10 per cent.

All the various measures undertaken by the design team would result in a fighter where all the initial costs had been strictly controlled. To illustrate this point, the tailplanes were interchangeable, as were the flaperons. A similar regime affected the main undercarriage units, most of whose components were also interchangeable. To reinforce the fact that this was a lightweight fighter, the avionics were simplified for the day-fighter role, while the armament was set at one 20-mm M61A1 rotary cannon, mounted in the left side of the fuselage, with a pair of AIM-9 Sidewinder missiles being carried, one per wing tip. The only other external extra was a pylon under each wing which had plumbing for external fuel tanks and wiring for other stores.

The culmination of all this effort was the roll-out of the prototype YF-16, 72-1567, at Fort Worth on 13 December 1973. Flight testing was to be carried out under USAF auspices.

Therefore, the YF-16 was dismantled and flown inside a C-5 Galaxy to Edwards AFB on 8 January 1974.

A surprising first flight

The first flight of the new fighter was completely inadvertent. During high-speed runs down the runway to test the various onboard systems, the pilot raised the nose slightly just short of rotate speed. Unfortunately a slight overcorrection of the nose resulted in the tailplanes scraping the runway. The resultant oscillation as the pilot tried to stop the aircraft taking off began to head towards the uncontrollable. Rather than lose the YF-16 before it had even flown, the pilot increased thrust and lifted the prototype gingerly off the runway. The resultant flight lasted all of six minutes and was flown with the gear down. During the post-flight debrief the test pilot reported that there were no significant handling problems. However, the damage caused to the right stabiliser during this inadvertent first flight meant that the official maiden flight was delayed. On 2 February 1974, 72-1567 undertook its official first flight, with test pilot Phil Oestricher at the controls. While airborne, the aircraft reached a speed of 644 km/h (400 mph) and an altitude of 9144 m (30,000 ft).

After the success of this first flight, it was not long before the second YF-16, 72-1568,

Lockheed Martin F-16C Block 50
52nd Fighter Wing

undertook its maiden flight. This took place on 9 March 1974, with test pilot Neil Anderson flying. Although both prototypes had flown with little incident, a fault came to light concerning the F100 engine. It had developed a tendency to revert to uncommanded idle while airborne, resulting in the pilot making a dead-stick landing. While the engineers investigated the fault, the YF-16s were placed under flight restrictions which kept them in sight of the airfield. Eventually, in-depth investigations traced the fault to microscopic metal particles contaminating the fuel control valves. These caused the valves to jam in the idle position.

With this fault ironed out, the competition fly-off between the YF-16s and the YF-17s could begin. Although the prototypes never flew directly against each other, they were matched against all the other aircraft in the USAF inventory. As well as dissimilar air combat tests, as many pilots as possible were given the opportunity to fly the aircraft, some engaging in mock dogfights against USAF-owned examples of the MiG-17 and -21. During these trials the YF-16s were reported to have reached speeds exceeding Mach 2, altitudes above 18288 m (60,000 ft) and loads up to 9 g during these manoeuvres.

Air Combat Fighter Program

Although both LWF aircraft were achieving or exceeding their laid down performance targets, the hierarchy within the USAF was still prejudiced against the programme, fearing that any success would weigh against the F-15 project. To allay the fears of the USAF, the Department of Defence (DoD) renamed the whole project as the Air Combat Fighter Program (ACF Program). Further pressure was also brought to bear by the European members of NATO, who had initiated the Multinational Fighter Programme Group (MFPG). This organisation had one aim – to find a replacement for the F-104G Starfighter which was coming to the end of its service life. Consisting of Belgium, Denmark, the Netherlands and Norway, the

working party had a shortlist of aircraft that consisted of the Dassault Mirage F1, General Dynamics YF-16, Northrop YF-17 and SAAB Viggen. What made the contest interesting was the proviso that the MFPG wanted a decision from the USAF concerning the ACF, before choosing its Starfighter replacement.

The US Navy also entered the fray, when a group of staff officers began to express doubts about the Grumman F-14 programme, which was running into problems and excessive cost overruns. This proposal became known as the VAFX, for which Grumman entered a stripped down version of the F-14. In May 1974, the House Armed Services Committee dictated that the US Navy would require a completely new aircraft and that the USAF should also buy into the programme, in theory to reduce procurement costs. What confounded the project from the outset, however, was that the services envisioned different roles for the VAFX. The Navy wanted it to cover both air and ground roles, while the Air Force only needed the aircraft for the air defence role. A few months later the US Congress diverted some of the VAFX money to fund a new project known as the Naval Air Combat Fighter, although to keep development costs down the technology already available from the USAF LWF/ACF programme was to be used wherever possible. It was at this point that the US Navy and USAF programmes split in two different directions.

In October 1974 the US Secretary of Defence (SecDef) James Schlesinger, announced that serious consideration would be given to production of the winner of the ACF contest, to satisfy the needs of the USAF, US Navy, NATO and other potential customers. To allay the fears of the USAF, Schlesinger stressed that the winner would complement the F-15 rather than replace it. The ACF would also become multi-role, complete with a BVR radar. The USAF was committed to purchasing 650 airframes, with a potential future buy of possibly 1,400 more.

The winner of the ACF contest was announced on 13 January 1975 by Air Force Secretary John

McLucas and was, as expected, the General Dynamics YF-16. Almost immediately, the USAF placed a contract for 15 full scale development (FSD) airframes, consisting of a mix of single-seaters designated F-16A and two-seaters designated F-16B. The official statement announcing the decision also highlighted the reasons behind it, these being lower operating costs, longer range and better handling qualities. A further advantage that swung the decision was the use of the F100 engine, which would power both the F-15 and the F-16. Politics also had a strong part to play, since General Dynamics was coming to the end of the F-111 programme and without the F-16 the Fort Worth company would be in dire trouble.

Fighting Falcons for NATO

With the USAF contract in place, the NATO consortium was offered the F-16 in February 1975, at a flyaway cost of $5.16 million per unit based on a total production run of 2,000 aircraft, although this would change when production offsets were introduced. To assist the programme, the US government cleared the technology involved in the F100 engine for export. This was not obviously a done deal, however, since none of the NATO countries had flown the type. To rectify this omission, the

FSD F-16 75-0750 is shown here complete with CCV fins under the intake. It was being used for AFTI trials work when this photograph was taken. *(C P Russell Smith Collection)*

YF-16 was flown across the Atlantic in May 1975 to undertake a sales tour throughout Europe, and to appear at the Paris Air Show. Having experienced the aircraft at first hand, and assured by the USAF order, the four European countries signed a memorandum of understanding (MoU) on 7 June 1975 for the F-16 to replace the F-104G. Contained within this memorandum was a definite initial order for 348 aircraft, which could be followed by more should the need arise.

As part of the production deal, a large consortium of Europe manufacturers was formed to absorb and apply the new technologies being offered as part of the F-16 programme. The primary contractors within Europe for final assembly were SABCA (Société Anonyme Belge de Constructions Aéronautiques), located at Gosselies in Belgium, and Fokker, based at Schipol. Manufacture of major sub-assemblies was undertaken at SONACA (Société Nationale de Construction Aérospatiale), once Fairey SA, which built the rear fuselages; Fokker, which constructed the centre section, flaperons and leading edge flaps; and SABCA, which manufactured much of the remainder. Further sub-assemblies, such as the fin, were built by Per Udsen in Denmark. The undercarriage was manufactured by DAF in the Netherlands, the matching wheels coming from the Norwegian firm Raufoss. Some minor assemblies were received from General Dynamics, Fort Worth, with some European-built assemblies going the other way.

Final construction of the European F100 engine was the responsibility of Fabrique National (FN) of Belgium, while in Norway Kongsberg was nominated to build the fin-mounted drive turbine modules. The remaining module, the augmentor nozzle, was the responsibility of Phillips Industries in Holland. Avionics were also split across the four partner nations, with MBLE based in Belgium having overall responsibility for the APG-66 radar system. The antenna for the APG-66 and the head-up display (HUD), were divested to Signaal and Oldeflt in Holland, while from Denmark came the fire control computer and radar display courtesy of Neselco, LK-NES and Nea Linberg. From Norway came the inertial navigation system which was to be manufactured by Kongsberg.

Production of the F-16 began at the Fort Worth plant in August 1975, after General Dynamics had undertaken an extensive refit of the plant that had been constructed for the manufacture of the Consolidated B-24 Liberator during World War Two. Comparing the YF-16 with the production model it was fairly obvious that some changes had been made. One of the most obvious was a fuselage extension of 33 cm (13 in)

One of the trials that 75-0751, the first FSD F-16B, was extensively involved in was the development of the type in the Wild Weasel role. To this end the aircraft sports a pair of Standard ARM missiles on the inner pylons, AGM-45 Shrikes on the outer pylons and ESM pods instead of Sidewinders on the wing tip rails. Also of note is the ECM pod on the centreline pylon. *(via USAF)*

An artist's impression of the first attempt to sell the F-16 to the US Navy. This was in response to the technical problems and cost overruns that were afflicting the Grumman F-14 Tomcat. In the event this programme only progressed as far as the drawing board. *(BBA Archive)*

and a reprofiled nose, which allowed for the installation of the Westinghouse APG-66 radar system, its associated avionics and a small increase in fuel load. Modifications were also undertaken to the wing, which was increased in area by 1.86 m² (20 sq ft), while some structural strengthening allowed for the fitment of four more pylons and their associated weaponry. This last modification brought the available number of pylons up to nine. Three each were under the wings, a single pylon was located under the fuselage and the remainder consisted of the wing tip missile rails. The primary pylons were rated for loads up to 4536 kg (10,000 lb). Two other modifications were also applied as production moved on, the first was a jet starter for the F100 engine, while the most obvious was an increase in tailplane size for better control throughout the flight envelope.

FSD reassessment

Prior to the appearance of the production F-16 a batch of FSD aircraft was to be constructed. As the two prototypes had proved the concept of the F-16, the need for 15 FSD airframes was reassessed down to six single-seat F-16As and two F-16Bs. These would be serialled 75-0745 to -0750 and 75-0751 and -0752 respectively. Construction proceeded quickly. Thus, the first F-16A/FSD made its maiden flight on 8 December 1976, flown by Neil Anderson. The first F-16B, the fourth FSD airframe, made its first flight on 8 August 1977, crewed by Neil Anderson and Phil Oestricher.

Soon after these successful maiden flights, the USAF announced that it would purchase a further 783 F-16s for use in the fighter-bomber role, a total contrast to the initial LWF specification, which was for a minimal day fighter. Production of the definitive F-16 began in

Europe at the SABCA plant in February 1978. It was quickly followed by the Fokker assembly line at Schipol in April 1978. To familiarise the Europeans with their new product, a Fort Worth production aircraft was delivered to Gosselies on 9 June 1978 for inspection and assembly training.

With Fiscal Year 1978 funding in place, large-scale production for the USAF began at General Dynamics, Fort Worth, with the first F-16A flying in August 1978. Europe was not far behind, as the first F-16 took to the air from Gosselies on 11 December 1978. This was an F-16B whose crew consisted of Neil Anderson representing General Dynamics and Serge Martin, representing the European consortium. The first flight of a Fokker-built F-16 for the Koninklijke Luchtmacht (KLu, Royal Netherlands Air Force) was undertaken on 3 May 1979.

The F-16 began to enter USAF service in January 1979, when the 388th TFW based at Hill AFB, Utah began to equip. In Europe the Belgian air force began to receive its aircraft during the same month, while the Netherlands received its first examples in June 1979. Deliveries of production machines to Norway and Denmark began in January 1980.

Even as production was building up in both

Europe and America, the Multinational Staged Improvement Program (MSIP) began. The object was to ensure that all building and in-service F-16s were modified and upgraded to the same common standard, thus ensuring cross compatibility of spares and servicing methods and standards.

And what of the pioneering aircraft? Of the YF-16s, the first prototype was later used in control configured vehicle (CCV) trials before retirement. The F-16A/FSD airframes were also used for numerous interesting trials. 75-0745 became the testbed for the General Electric F101

engine, before retiring to the USAF Museum at Wright-Patterson AFB. Airframe -0747 was extensively modified with a cranked-arrow wing to become the F-16XL/B. After initial flight trials the aircraft was transferred to NASA as 848. A further aircraft, -0749, was modified to F-16XL/A standard, complete with cranked-arrow wing. It too was transferred to NASA, being numbered 849. The last single-seat FSD aircraft, -0750, was modified as the AFTI (Advanced Fighter Technology Integration) testbed. Of the two-seaters, only -0752 was used in trials work. Its first role was as a testbed for the projected Wild Weasel defence suppression version, after which it was modified to act as the testbed for the General Electric J79 engine as the F-16/79.

This offset rear shot is of the NASA-operated VISTA F-16 two-seater, which is engaged in flight trials of numerous airframe and engine technologies. *(NASA)*

2. Operational History

Since the Lockheed Martin/General Dynamics F-16 has become a staple in the ranks of many of the world's air forces, the entry for each operator is by necessity brief. We start within NATO, with the Belgian air force (BAF), or Force Aérienne Belge/Belgische Luchmacht, which was the first recipient of the European-built aircraft. Constructed at the SABCA plant at Gosselies, the first BAF machine, a two-seater serialled FB-01, was delivered on 29 January 1979. The original order for 116 aircraft comprised 96 F-16As and 20 F-16B twin-seaters. Initial operating capability (IOC) was achieved by the BAF in January 1981, by which time 23 aircraft had been delivered.

The early batches of machines were built to Block 1/5 standard although they would later be upgraded to Block 10 status. By the time the 56th aircraft was on the production line, the F-16s were being constructed to Block 15 standard,

Lined up for touchdown on the runway at RAF Waddington, this BAF F-16A sports an ACMI (air-combat manoeuvring instrumentation) pod on its wing tip rail, a dummy AIM-9 under the wing and a green-painted ECM pod on the centreline pylon. *(C P Russell Smith Collection)*

Esk 730 provided this F-16A, E-191, for display purposes in the early 1990s. The AIM-9s on the aircraft's wing tips sported sharkmouths and the Danish unit's identity. *(BBA Archive)*

complete with enlarged tailplanes. This initial order was followed by a top-up/attrition replacement batch of 44 aircraft authorised in February 1983. Deliveries began in March 1987 and were completed in 1991.

BAF aircraft differ from those of many other nations in that they have an internal ESD Carapace electronic countermeasures (ECM) system fitted, this resulting in the deletion of the normal undernose aerials. Another change from the standard F-16 was the installation of brake chutes in the tails of the final 44 aircraft, a modification later embodied in the survivors. Weaponry has also been experimented with as the MATRA Magic 2 missile underwent evaluation as a possible replacement or supplement to the AIM-9 Sidewinder. Although the trials were successful, the missile has not been adopted as a standard.

In June 1993, the Belgian government committed itself to the MLU (Mid-Life Update) programme. Intended initially to cover some 48 aircraft, the upgrade involved a major avionics overhaul with the installation of a global positioning system (GPS), microwave landing system (MLS), advanced identification friend or foe (IFF) and an improved radar system.

The air force has also undergone a major reshuffle, with Tactical Air Force Command being reduced from three wings to two, consisting of six squadrons of 12 aircraft each.

The remaining early-build F-16A/B aircraft have been withdrawn from service and placed in long term storage at Weelde airfield. Attempts have been made to sell these aircraft, however, since there is a glut of early-build F-16s available for sale worldwide, it is more likely that some will be employed as instructional airframes while the remainder are used as spares sources.

In Belgian service the following units have flown the F-16A/B: No. 1 Smaldeel/Escadrille, No. 2 Wing, Florennes AB; No. 2 Smaldeel/Escadrille, Kleine-Brogel AB; No. 23 Smaldeel/Escadrille, part of No. 10 Wing; No. 31 Smaldeel/Escadrille; and Nos 349 and 350 Smaldeel/Escadrille and the Operational Conversion Squadron (OCS) at Beauvechain. As the force realignment continues, the OCS and No. 350 Smaldeel/Escadrille are scheduled to move to Kleine-Brogel.

Denmark

Denmark is another country within the NATO framework that decided to replace its Starfighters with the F-16. The initial contract was for 40 F-16As and 12 F-16Bs, production being undertaken at Gosselies. On 18 February 1980 the first F-16A was delivered to Eskadrille (Esk) 727, with the last arriving in 1984. To replace attrition losses and to provide spares, a further batch of 12 aircraft was ordered in 1984. Consisting of eight F-16As and four F-16Bs, these machines were fitted with the larger tailplanes and came from the Fokker line. As with the Belgian machines those of the Royal Danish Air Force (RDAF), or Kongelige Danske Flyvevaaben), underwent an upgrade programme, known as *Pacer Loft 1*, which was applied to Block 1/5 machines. Once the first ten had been completed, a further dozen were slated for updating during 1989, but this plan fell foul of the defence spending cuts which also saw the disbandment of the Danish Saab Draken squadrons. In RDAF service seven machines have been lost in accidents, although there have been some replacements in the shape of three ex-USAF F-16s which have been updated to the same standard as the remaining aircraft.

With afterburner shock rings in its wake this F-16A, J-003 of the Royal Netherlands Air Force, blasts off to begin another display. Among F-16 operators, the KLu has consistently produced the most colourful display aircraft year on year. *(C P Russell Smith Collection)*

In RDAF service, the F-16 is operated by Nos 723, 726, 727 and 730 Eskadrilles, based at Aalborg; while Skrydstrup AB is home to Esk 727, the first unit to equip, and Esk 730, which acts as the pilot conversion unit. Reconnaissance duties are the responsibility of Esk 726.

Netherlands

Alongside Belgium, Denmark and Norway, the Netherlands also elected to join the launch of the international F-16 programme. Operating in conjunction with SABCA, a second production line was established by Fokker in Holland. The initial contract called for 102 machines, although this soon grew to 213 after the second batch was confirmed in December 1983. First deliveries to the Koninklijke Luchtmacht (KLu) began on 7 June 1979 when the initial machine arrived at Leeuwarden. The final Dutch F-16 was delivered in March 1992.

Assigned to the 2nd Allied Tactical Air Force (ATAF), there were initially nine front-line KLu F-16 squadrons, although changes within the Soviet Union and a restructuring of the KLu saw this total reduced to six, based at three bases instead of the earlier five. A follow on from this reduction saw the early-model F-16s being withdrawn from service. Various scenarios have been postulated for their disposal including resale, their reduction for spares and their retention for instructional use, the latter two being favoured. The aircraft of the KLu have been undergoing the MLU programme.

One of the earliest units to receive the F-16 was No. 306 Squadron (Sqn) at Volkel AB which is tasked with a multitude of roles. These include tactical reconnaissance using the Orpheus pod, aircraft so-equipped being designated F-16A(R), and close air support. The unit is part of No. 2 ATAF and the NATO Rapid Reaction Force. It is this latter commitment that ensures that the aircraft and crews of No. 306 Sqn, plus those of Nos 315 and 322 Sqns, are fully occupied in duties involving reinforcing the no-fly zones over Iraq. Other units within the KLu that operate the F-16 include No. 312 Sqn, Volkel AB; No. 313 Sqn, Twenthe AB; No. 314 Sqn, since disbanded; No. 315 Sqn, Twenthe AB and Nos 316 and 323 Sqns, both since disbanded.

Norway

Norway was the last of the four NATO countries to specify the F-16 as a replacement for the F-104G. When the decision was made to accept the F-16, a total of 72 was envisaged as enough to satisfy the country's defence requirement. Placed with Fokker, the Norwegian contract called for 60 F-16As and 12 F-16Bs. The first delivery to the Royal Norwegian Air Force (RNoAF), or Kongelige Norske Luftforsvaret, was undertaken during December 1979, with the final machine arriving in June 1984. Unlike their

In the main the F-16s of the Royal Norwegian Air Force keep their unit marks to the bare minimum as this example from No. 332 Skv reveals. Even the roundels are as small as possible. *(BBA Archive)*

more southerly counterparts, the Norwegian aircraft were equipped from the outset with a brake chute, in an extended tail cone, to improve stopping performance on ice- and snow-covered runways. The primary role of the Norwegian aircraft is air defence, while their secondary role is coastal defence. For the latter, the Penguin

Mk 3 anti-shipping missile is deployed. During its use of the F-16, the RNoAF has lost 14 aircraft to a number of causes, but has been able to replace no more than two due to cuts in the defence budget.

The four units that fly the F-16 in Norway are Nos 331, 332, 334 and 338 Skvadrons based at Bodo, Rygge, Bodo and Orland respectively. In

Outbound on a training sortie, this Greek F-16D sports a triple-ejector rack (TER) on the outer wing pylon, although in this instance no weapons are carried. *(C P Russell Smith Collection)*

1984. the latter unit became the last to form on the type. Of the other three units, No. 334 Skvadron is primarily charged with deploying the locally built Kongsberg Penguin Mk 3, while the remaining units provide the nation's air defence.

Greece

With the USA and four European NATO countries as confirmed customers for the F-16 it came as no surprise that other countries would choose the type. One of the first nations to do so was Greece, which made its intentions known in November 1984. Intended to provide a replacement for the Northrop F-5 Freedom Fighter, the F-16 contract was signed in January 1987, with the first aircraft being handed over on 18 November 1988. The final machine of the 42-strong order was delivered in October 1989, by which time the Hellenic air force, or Elliniki Aeroporia, had received 34 Block 30 F-16Cs and six F-16Ds. The receiving unit for the *Peace Xenia* programme aircraft was 111 Pterix (Wing) whose

two squadrons, Nos 330 and 346 Mira, are based at Nea Ankhialos AB. A further 40 machines were ordered for delivery during 1997/98. These aircraft were to Block 50 standard and were intended to finally replace the remaining F-5s.

Portugal

As more F-16C/Ds have become available for use by more affluent nations, their unwanted F-16A/Bs have been put up for resale to countries with smaller budgets. One of the recipients of this largesse was the Portuguese air force, or Força Aérea Portuguesa (FAP), which applied to the US Congress in June 1990 for 20 F-16A/Bs to replace the LTV A-7P Corsair IIs that it employed in the air defence role. Originally intended for 1992 delivery, the original order was replaced by a new requirement for new-build Block 15OCU aircraft, the first of which were handed over in July 1994. The unit that now flies the F-16 is Esquadra 201 based at Monte Real.

F-16A 15102 of the FAP was photographed as it prepared to depart for a training sortie. Underwing the aircraft has an SUU-20A pod, which carries smoke and flash bombs, plus a limited quantity of machine-gun ammunition. (C P Russell Smith Collection)

Turkey

Turkey has not only become an F-16 operator, the country has also gained a manufacturing capability that allows it to produce complete aircraft for sale to third parties. Plans to purchase the F-16 were first announced in September 1983, when a requirement for 160 of the type consisting of 132 F-16Cs and 28 F-16Ds, was identified. The intention was that the Turkish air force, or Turk Hava Kuvvetleri (THK), would replace its ageing fighter fleets with the new type. Eventually the order was increased to 240 machines which will allow the THK to replace all of its F-4 Phantoms. Turkey will then be able to standardise on one aircraft for its multi-role requirements.

The first F-16s were delivered to Turkey in kit form during March 1985 for study prior to Tusas Aerospace Industries (TAI), the local aircraft manufacturer, constructing its own machines. The first flight of a locally built F-16 was undertaken on 20 October 1987. The initial delivery programme to the THK was titled *Peace Onyx I* and began in October 1987, when the first 44 aircraft were delivered to No. 141 Filo, part of No. 4 Ana Jet Us (AJU). These first machines were to Block 30 standard, while the remainder

On the runway threshold awaiting final clearance, this pair of THK F-16Ds is part of the inventory of No. 151 Filo/No. 5 AJU based at Merzifon AB. *(Bob Archer/BBA Archive)*

are to the far more capable Block 40/50 configuration complete with LANTIRN capability. The Block 40/50 programme was designated *Peace Onyx II.*

In service the F-16C/D equips four units, the first of these being No. 4 AJU whose flying components are Nos 141 and 142 Filos, based at Akinci AB. Also based here is the Oncel Filo, whose main task is conversion. Since their entry into service, the Block 30 machines have been upgraded with improved ECM equipment.

No. 6 AJU, whose flying components are Nos 161 and 162 Filos, based at Bandirma AB, flies the more advanced F-16 Block 40. Deliveries took place between May 1991 and May 1993, with LANTIRN pod integration being slated for February 1994. No. 8 AJU, whose flying units are Nos 181 and 182 Filos, based at Diyarbakir AB, equipped with the F-16 Block 40 in early 1994. The final Wing to re-equip with the F-16 was No. 9 AJU, whose units are Nos 191 and 192 Filos, based at Balikesir AB. Since reaching operational status, the Wing has provided both crews and aircraft for Operation *Deny Flight*, a detachment operating from Ghedi-Brecia AB in Italy under UN mandate.

Bahrain

The F-16 has also proved popular in the Middle East. A surprise buy was that by Bahrain in 1987, as part of the *Peace Crown* programme.

Consisting of 12 F-16C/Ds powered by the GE F110 engine, first deliveries took place in March 1990. In service they supplemented the Bahrain Amiri Air Force's single squadron of Northrop F-5E/F Tiger II fighters. After the 1990 invasion of Kuwait, the aircraft of the Bahrain Amiri AF were assigned to operations within the *Desert Storm* coalition framework. This participation enabled Bahrain to become a recipient of low cost arms sales from America.

Egypt

In 1979, the government of Egypt signed a peace treaty with Israel, ending 30 years of hostility and warfare. As one of the benefits of this agreement, Egypt became a major recipient of American military aid. On 25 June 1980, Egypt signed a letter of agreement to acquire 42 F-16A/B Block 15 fighters, consisting of 34 F-16As and eight F-16Bs, under the *Peace Vector* FMS (Foreign Military Sales) programme. The first F-16 was accepted by the Egyptian air force (EAF), or Al Quwwat al Jawwiya Ilmisriya, in January 1982.

A year later, Egypt ordered 40 additional F-16C/Ds, consisting of 34 F-16Cs and six F-16Ds. These are to Block 32 standard, and after a retrofit, are some of the few examples of F-16C/D compatible with the AIM-7 Sparrow. In October 1986, the first F-16C arrived in Egypt under *Peace Vector II*. The 242nd Regiment at Beni Suef began operating F-16C/Ds in October 1986. By 1997, all Block 32 aircraft had been modified to Block 42 standard.

In June 1990, Egypt confirmed a contract for 35 F-16C Block 40 and 12 F-16D Block 40 aircraft powered by the GE F110 engine. This order was under *Peace Vector III*, and these aircraft were intended to equip two squadrons, as well as to make up for attrition losses. The first *Peace Vector III* F-16s were delivered in October 1991.

A further contract to produce F-16C/D Block 40s for the EAF was placed with TAI, covering 46 machines, 34 of them F-16Cs and 12 F-16Ds. This deal was carried out under the auspices of *Peace Vector IV*, and marked the first

sale of a foreign-built F-16 to a third-party nation. The first aircraft was delivered in early 1994, and deliveries continued into 1995. For formal bureaucratic reasons concerning the regulations under which the FMS programme operates, TAI is not allowed to deliver F-16s directly to Egypt. Instead, the aircraft are initially delivered to the USAF, which then turns them over to the recipient.

In May 1996, the governments of Egypt and America signed an agreement providing for the sale of 21 new F-16C/D Block 40 aircraft to the EAF. The contract is worth $670 million. This was Egypt's fifth order for F-16s over the last 15 years. The contract was fulfilled at Fort Worth, with deliveries beginning in 1999. The selected engine was the F110-GE-100B.

In June 1999, the Egypt ordered a further 24 new build F-16 Block 40s. These aircraft were delivered in 2001–2002 as the last Block 40s to be manufactured.

Since entering service with Egypt, the older F-16C/D aircraft have been modified in-country through Engineering Change Proposals detailing requirements for the installation and integration of Harpoon missiles and GBU-15 electro-optically guided bombs, radar modifications and changes to other related systems. Principal contractors for the upgrade programme were McDonnell Douglas, Rockwell International (Tactical Systems Division) and the Westinghouse Electronic Systems Group.

All aircraft in the Block 15 and 32 series are in the process of being upgraded to Block 42 standard, retaining the P&W F100 engine and associated small intake. The modifications scheduled for the Egyptian F-16 Block 40/42 allow the aircraft to use LANTIRN pods, since they have been modified with the larger holographic HUD, these changes allowing autonomous use of laser-guided bombs (LGBs).

Four Tactical Fighter Brigades (TFBs) of the EAF now operate the F-16. No. 232 TFB operates Block 42-standard aircraft (modified Block 15s), No. 242 TFB flies modified Block 32 aircraft (now upgraded to Block 42 standard), No. 262 TFB

The IDF/AF has been an enthusiastic F-16 operator since the type's earliest days. Festooned with weaponry, F-16A 299, of the flight trials unit, awaits its next sortie. *(C P Russell Smith Collection)*

flies the US-built Block 40 aircraft and No. 272 TFB flies the Turkish-built Block 40s.

Israel

The Israel Defence Force/Air Force (IDF/AF), or Heyl Ha'Avir, got its first chance to test the F-16 with the 388th TFW at Hill AFB, this being the first USAF unit operational on type. The IDF/AF test team subsequently recommended the purchase of the Fighting Falcon. In August 1978, the Carter Administration's arms-sales restrictions policy had come to an end, allowing Israel to announce plans to acquire F-16A/Bs. The fact that Israel had just signed the Camp David peace accords with Egypt however swung the deal and the request was approved.

The first F-16 was handed over on 31 January 1980, subsequently being flown to Hill AFB, where initial pilot and ground crew conversion took place. The first deliveries to Israel took place under the *Peace Marble I* programme. These aircraft were originally intended for the Imperial Iranian Air Force, but the fall of the Shah in 1979 and the consequent rise of a fundamentalist Islamic regime, caused them to be diverted to Israel.

The machines delivered to Israel had a number of changes that were unique, including the fitting of chaff/flare dispensers. The first four F-16s, known as Netz (Hawk) in IDF/AF service, arrived in Israel in July 1980. IOC was achieved a few weeks later.

After *Peace Marble I* came *Peace Marble II*, under which the IDF/AF was supplied with Block 30 F-16C/D Fighting Falcons, the first of which arrived in October 1987. A total of 75 Block 30 aircraft was delivered: 51 F-16Cs known locally as Baraks (Lightnings) and 24 F-16Ds known as Brakeets (Thunderbolts).

Following the cancellation of the indigenous IAI Lavi fighter project in May 1988, a follow-on order was placed for 60 Block 40 F-16C/Ds, plus an unexercised option for 15 more, all being delivered under *Peace Marble III*. The first of these F-16s arrived in Israel in August 1991. In recognition of its restraint during the 1991 Gulf War, Israel was provided with 50 surplus USAF F-16A/Bs to Block 10 standard, the first of these being delivered in August 1994 under the *Peace Marble IV* programme. Deliveries ended in late 1994.

In January 2000, Israel ordered further F-16s, in the shape of the so-called F-16I. Some 50 F-16D Block 52+ aircraft, plus an option for 60 further machines, were covered by the contract. Delivery of the firm-order aircraft is scheduled for 2003–2006 under *Peace Marble V*, while the optioned machines could be delivered in 2006–2008. Due to security restrictions very little is known concerning the actual units that fly the F-16, although the following are known to have used the type at some time: Nos 101, 109, 110, 117, 140, 144, 190 and 253 Sqns.

Jordan

In July 1994, King Hussein of Jordan signed a peace treaty with Israel, bringing to an end 40 years of hostility. Shortly afterwards, the Jordanian government began to lobby the American government for approval to purchase as many as 42 F-16A/B aircraft. The result was a $220-million agreement signed between the USA and Jordan on 29 July 1996. It authorised the lease of 16 F-16s, consisting of 12 F-16As and four F-16Bs. This agreement, formally signed by Field Marshal Marei, Chief of Staff (CoS) of the Royal Jordanian Armed Forces and Major General Ababneh, CoS of the Royal Jordanian Air Force (RJAF), was linked to the Middle East peace process and closer US-Jordanian relations.

The complete package, known as the *Peace Falcon* Program, includes funding for structural upgrades, engine modifications, support equipment, spare parts procurement and all training. The agreement constituted two lease contracts and a Letter of Offer and Acceptance. The first was a no-cost lease, covering 13 F-16A/B Block 15 Air Defence Fighter (ADF) aircraft. Under the Arms Export Control Act, the DoD was able to provide these aircraft on a no-cost lease because they had flown over 75 per cent of their life. Three of the B-model aircraft still had more than 25 per cent of their life left, however, and they fall under the second $4.5 million lease. Both leases covered a five-year period.

The official roll-out of the first *Peace Falcon* aircraft was on 28 October 1997 at Hill AFB. The delivery schedule for the programme required that six aircraft be available for ferry to Jordan in December 1997, with the remainder due in January/February 1998. Eventually, the RJAF would like to acquire as many as 70 F-16s –

enough to equip three squadrons. In service the aircraft are used solely in the air defence role, being based at Mujaq Al-Sath AB with No. 2 Sqn. The aircraft are armed only with AIM-9s, but there are hopes that AIM-120 AMRAAM (Advanced Medium-Range Air-to-Air Missile) can be acquired.

United Arab Emirates

In September 1996, the government of the United Arab Emirates (UAE) notified Lockheed Martin that the F-16 and the Dassault Rafale had been selected as final candidates in the UAE's new fighter competition. Lockheed Martin had offered a range of F-16 configurations for consideration, one of which was the Block 60, incorporating the F-16ES's conformal fuel tanks and integral FLIR. The UAE had linked any potential order to the availability of the AIM-120 as well as offsets, requirements that were a prerequisite for awarding the contract. On 12 May 1998, the government of the UAE announced that it had selected Lockheed Martin's new F-16 Block 60 as its advanced fighter aircraft. The programme, including 80 aircraft, weapons, and support is valued at approximately $7 billion. A contract was signed in 2000 and deliveries are expected to begin in 2004, for completion in 2006.

Indonesia

The Far East and Asia have also been ready markets for the F-16. The first such customer was Indonesia, which signed a Letter of Intent in August 1986 for 12 F-16A/B Block 15OCU aircraft. They were intended to replace some of the ageing MiG-21 'Fishbed' fighters and other Soviet types that were in Indonesian service. The first F-16 was delivered to the Tentara Nasional Indonesia-Angkatan Udara, or Indonesian air force, in December 1989, under the *Peace Bima-Sena* programme. Deliveries were completed in 1990.

In March 1996, the Indonesian air force CoS, Air Vice-Marshal Sutria Tubagus, signed a contract with Lockheed Martin for procurement

Although at first sight this appears to be a USAF F-16C, it is in fact an aircraft belonging to the Republic of Singapore Air Force, as the national insignia reveals. It is based at Luke AFB for the training of RSAF pilots. *(Scott Van Aken)*

of an additional nine F-16A Block 20s. These aircraft had originally been manufactured for Pakistan, but were embargoed under the Pressler amendment to the Foreign Assistance Act, which forbids military aid to any nation possessing a nuclear explosive device. All of the F-16s are assigned to No. 3 Sqn at Ishwahyudi AB, although half of the F-16 inventory doubles as a demonstration team, the 'Blue Falcons'. Further procurement of the F-16 has been stalled owing to alleged human rights abuses.

Pakistan

Another country that has endured arms embargoes is Pakistan. In this case the embargo was enforced in the light of the possibility of the country possessing nuclear weapons. In December 1981, the government of Pakistan signed a letter of agreement for the purchase of 40 F-16A/B aircraft, consisting of 28 F-16As and 12 F-16Bs for the Pakistan air force (PAF), or Pakistan Fiza'ya. The first aircraft were accepted in October 1982, the first landing in Pakistan occurring at Sargodha Air Base on 15 January 1983.

The Pakistani F-16A/Bs are all Block 15 aircraft, the final version of the F-16A/B production run, and are powered by the F100-PW-200 turbofan. All 40 aircraft were delivered between 1983 and 1987. Ten years later, at least eight aircraft of the initial *Peace Gate I* order had been lost in accidents with no replacements forthcoming, although the remainder are being supported by other agencies outside of the USA.

In December 1988, Pakistan ordered 11 additional F-16A/B Block 15OCU aircraft, consisting of six F-16As and five F-16Bs, under *Peace Gate II*. These aircraft were purchased as much needed attrition replacements and fully paid for, but were embargoed and placed into storage at the Aircraft Maintenance and Regeneration Center in Arizona.

Pakistan has steadfastly refused to sign the Nuclear Non-proliferation Treaty. As a result, in accordance with the Pressler amendment, the US government announced in October 1990 that it had embargoed further arms deliveries. This, however, is not the end of the story, since the US has now restored trade links with the country. This could result in deliveries of new-build aircraft. In PAF service the surviving F-16s are flown by Nos 9, 11 and 14 Sqns based at Sargodha and Kamra ABs.

Singapore

The government of Singapore ordered eight F-16/79 fighters in January 1985, with an option for 12 more. The F-16/79 was a cheaper version of the F-16 powered by the GE J79 turbojet, rather than the F100 turbofan. In mid-1985, it became apparent that the F100-powered version would be made available, however, and Singapore changed its order to eight F-16A/B Block 15OCU aircraft, consisting of four F-16As and four F-16Bs. This purchase was made under the auspices of *Peace Carvin*, and was intended to allow replacement of the ageing Hawker Hunters still serving with the Republic of Singapore Air Force (RSAF). Singapore took delivery of its first F100-PW-220-powered F-16 on 20 February 1988. Although all the aircraft are Block 15 models, they actually have strengthened Block 30 airframes. The machines were initially delivered to Luke AFB, where the RSAF trains its F-16 pilots.

In 1994, when a *Peace Carvin III* order for 18 Block 52 F-16C/D aircraft was announced, it was revealed that the F-16A/Bs would be sold once the C/Ds were operational, as the earlier machines were seen as too expensive to operate logistically. A further 12 Block 52 C/Ds were ordered in 1997 for delivery in 1999/2000, with another 20 similar machines being ordered in late 2000 for delivery in the timescale 2003–2005. Finally, Singapore has also leased F-16s for training in the US. These include nine ex-USAF F-16A/Bs for use at Luke from 1993–1996 and 12 Block 42 aircraft from 1996–1998. From late 1998, 12 new-build Block 52s have been in use at Cannon AFB, New Mexico. In service, the front-line F-16s serve with Nos 140 and 143 Sqns at Tengah AB.

Republic of Korea

The Republic of Korea faces a heavily armed and intransigent North Korea, equipped with at least 600 tactical jet aircraft. In December 1981, the Republic of Korea signed a letter of agreement for the purchase of 36 F-16C/D Block 32s under the *Peace Bridge* programme. This made the Republic of Korea Air Force (RoKAF) the first foreign operator of the F-16C/D. These aircraft were to augment F-4D/E Phantoms and F-5E Tiger IIs, which were at that time the primary combat aircraft serving with the RoKAF.

The Korean F-16 programme was christened Victory Falcon in 1986 by Chun Doo Hwan, President of the Republic of Korea. Because there were still funds remaining after *Peace Bridge*, a further four F-16D Block 32s were ordered in June 1988. Further F-16s on order for the RoKAF will be assembled in country.

Photographs of RoKAF aircraft are quite rare, since Korea is by nature a secretive country. This machine, 054, an F-16C, has been parked with its airbrakes partly open. Alongside is the F-16 specific boarding ladder which clips into specially designed recesses in the airframe. *(C P Russell Smith Collection)*

Taiwan

In November 1992, Taiwan and the US signed an agreement for the sale of 150 F-16A/B aircraft, consisting of 120 A-models and 30 B-models, to Taiwan under the *Peace Fenghuang* programme. All are F-16 Block 15OCUs, built to MLU specifications.

At the start of 1997, five aircraft were formally handed over to Taiwan, with the first two F-16s arriving at Chiayi AB on 14 April 1997. The deliveries will continue at a rate of approximately two per month, until all 150 aircraft are delivered, an event which took place in 1999. In service, the F-16s are based at Chiayi AB where the 4th Tactical Fighter Wing is established with 60 aircraft. The first operational unit was the 21st Tactical Fighter Squadron (TFS), with the second, the 22nd TFS, achieving

operational status on 23 July 1998. Tao Yuan AB will become the second home base for the 401st Combined Tactical Wing consisting of three F-16 fighter units and one F-16 squadron equipped with reconnaissance pods.

Thailand

Thailand has suffered financial problems in recent years, but in April 1985 its government felt secure enough to ask the US for 12 F-16A/Bs. Later, following a letter of agreement signed in December 1987 six further F-16s were delivered. In September 1995, Thailand received the first aircraft of a third batch of 18 new F-16A/B Block 15OCU aircraft, consisting of 12 A models and six B models. In Royal Thai Air Force service the fighters are operated by Nos 103 and 403 Squadrons at Korat AB.

Toting a full warload of AIM-120 missiles, rockets and fuel tanks, this F-16CG also sports a LANTIRN pod under the intake. This aircraft, 89-001, is bedecked in the colours of the 31st FW, based at Aviano AB, Italy. Aviano is possibly the most important F-16 base in the world. *(Nick Challoner)*

Venezuela

At the moment Venezuela is the only country in Latin America to operate the F-16, although Chile is currently negotiating for a quantity. In May 1982, the government of Venezuela signed an agreement to purchase 18 Block 15 F-16As and six Block 15 F-16Bs to replace the fleet of Mirage III/5 fighters serving with the Venezuelan air force, or Fuerza Aérea Venezolana (FAV). This purchase, under the *Peace Delta* programme, took longer than expected to be approved because the US government initially wished to sell Venezuela the F-16/79.

However, in 1983, the US finally approved the sale of the F100-powered F-16 to Venezuela, and the first aircraft was accepted by the FAV in September 1983. In service the main operator is Grupo Aero de Caza No. 16, which oversees Escuadron 161 'Caribes' and Escuadron 162 'Gavilanes', both at El Libertador AB, Palo Negro.

United States

For a nation that at first decried the F-16 as a front-line fighter, the United States has eventually accepted the greatest quantity from the production lines. The USAF accepted its first F-16 on 17 August 1978, with the first unit to equip being the 388th TFW at Hill AFB, Utah. Although designated as a front-line unit, the primary purpose of the 388th was to train crews for Tactical Air Command (TAC) and for those foreign customers that required training support.

In USAF service the F-16 now serves with, or has served with, the following units: 8th Fighter Wing (FW), Kunsan AB, South Korea; 18th FW, Kadena AB, Okinawa, Japan; 31st FW, Homestead AFB, Florida; 50th TFW, Hahn AB, Germany; 51st FW, Osan AB, South Korea; 52nd FW, Spangdahlem AB, Germany; 56th FW, MacDill AFB, Florida; 57th Wing, Nellis AFB, Florida; 81st TFW, RAF Bentwaters (since disbanded); 86th FW, Ramstein AB, Germany; 347th FW, Moody AFB, Georgia; 354th FW, Eilson AFB, Alaska; 363rd FW, Shaw AFB, South Carolina; 366th FW, Mountain Home AFB, Idaho; 388th FW, Hill AFB, Utah; 401st TFW, Torrejon AB, Spain (since disbanded); 432nd FW, Misawa AB, Japan; 474th TFW, Nellis AB, Nevada (since disbanded); 3246th Test Wing (TW), Eglin AFB, Florida; 6510th TW, Edwards AFB, California; Tactical Air Warfare Center, Eglin AFB,

The F-16CG Block 40 is the only F-16 model with night and all-weather navigation and precision-attack capabilities. Its mission is to find the target and drop guided bombs such as the GBU-10/12/24 LGB. The F-16CG uses the Low-Altitude Navigation and Targeting Infra-Red for Night (LANTIRN) system to find targets at night or in bad weather. This particular machine is part of the 51st Wing based at Osan AB, Korea. *(Bob Archer/BBA Archive)*

The Miramar-based 'Top Gun' F-16Ns not only sported grey/blue camouflage schemes, but they also appeared in desert colours as this machine shows. *(Scott Van Aken)*

Florida and the Ogden Air Logistics Center, Hill AFB, Utah.

Recognising the value of the Air Force Reserve (AFRES) as an adjunct to the regular Air Force, great efforts have been made to improve the equipment that the organisation operates. The first AFRES unit to equip with the F-16 was the 419th TFW based at Hill AFB, which received its first aircraft in January 1984. After the 419th came the 310th TFW, Carswell AFB, Texas; 482nd TFW, Homestead AFB, Florida; 507th TFG, Tinker AFB, Oklahoma; 906th TFG, Wright-Patterson AFB, Ohio; 924th FW, Bergstrom AFB, Texas; 926th FW, Naval Air Station (NAS) New Orleans and the 944th TFG, Luke AFB, Arizona.

Another group of part timer flyers that has began to reap the benefits of new aircraft is the Air National Guard (ANG). Although controlled on a state basis, in times of need the command of ANG units devolves to the Federal Government. The first ANG unit to receive the F-16 was the 169th TFG/South Carolina ANG in July 1983. Eventually the ANG received more than 800 F-16s, which allowed a further 38 units to re-equip with the type.

Dissimilar Air Combat Training (DACT) is a vital role for all air forces and the USN is no exception. It has operated a variety of aircraft in the DACT role, including the F-16N. Based on the standard F-16C/D, the F-16N has no internal cannon, missile-firing capability or onboard ECM. However, it was compatible with air combat manoeuvring instrumentation pods (ACMI) for data transmission. Such a pod would normally be located on a wing tip missile rail. The F-16N also had a much strengthened wing to cater for the increased *g* regularly pulled during DACT manoeuvres.

The F-16N was delivered to the Navy during the period 1987 to mid-1988, the first unit so equipped being VF-126 at NAS Miramar, with IOC being achieved in April 1987. A further two units, VF-43 and VF-45, also received the F-16N. Eventually a total of 22 F-16Ns and four TF-16N two-seaters was delivered. In 1994, the situation regarding the DACT requirement and its funding changed, with VF-43 and VF-126 disbanding. Although VF-45 and the Fighter Weapons School still nominally operate the F-16N, it is reported that the aircraft are actually held in flyable storage awaiting funding for repairs, before reinstatement or resale. Interestingly, during 2002 the US Navy revealed that it would be receiving a number of the embargoed Pakistani F-16A/Bs for aggressor training.

3. Combat Operations

The concept behind the F-16 surfaced in 1965 as the ADF/LWF project in response to developing technologies in both the US and the USSR. This role had already been partly filled by the Northrop F-5 series, however, it was felt that this design was not capable of further improvement without a total revamp. Soon, the Vietnam War had changed the perceptions of the USAF and it abandoned the ADF/LWF idea for far more complex machines, that suffered from rising costs and required extensive nursing to keep flying.

Fortunately for the USAF and other air forces around the world two men continued to push the ADF idea, sometimes against the flow of command opinion. Major John Boyd, a former USAF fighter instructor, and Pierre Sprey, a civilian weapons specialist working in the office of the Assistant Secretary of Defense for Systems Analysis, worked together to convince the Pentagon that pushing forward with the more complicated F-X programme alone would leave the US vulnerable to attack. Further support came from Lt-Col Everest Riccioni, USAF, and other pilots, who were determined to push for an alternative to the complicated F-X.

The first country to take the F-16 to war was Israel, when it carried out a successful strike against a nuclear reactor building near Baghdad. The aircraft illustrated is allocated to the IDF/AF Test Establishment and carries a reasonable load of training bombs. *(C P Russell Smith Collection)*

A change of president after Richard Nixon was elected saw Deputy Defense Secretary David A. Packard helping to bring the ADF to fruition, when he authorised the RFP in January 1971. Determination of the best design was under the guidance of Lt-Gen. James Stewart of the Source Selection Authority. It rated the General Dynamics and Northrop designs as worthy for consideration. In contest with the other manufacturers, General Dynamics had put forward a successful submission that clinched a development contract for the new fighter, with the final authorisation being made by Secretary of the Air Force Robert C. Seamans.

Known as the Model 401 and designated as the YF-16, design and development of this $37.9 million project was concentrated at Fort Worth, Texas. The directors of design were William C. Dietz and Lyman C. Josephs, while the chief designer was Harry Hillaker. All three would be heavily involved in refining the design before the first prototype was rolled out for public view on 13 December 1973. Test flying

Caught just at the moment of touch-down at a wet Aviano AB, this F-16C has just returned from a CAP over the former Yugoslavia. *(USAF)*

was undertaken at Edwards AFB, the pilot involved being Phil Oestricher, who discovered an unusual way of carrying out the first unofficial flight during a high speed taxi run. The official maiden flight was carried out by the same pilot on 2 February 1974. Following on from the initial YF-16 came the second, which was piloted by Neil Anderson on 9 March 1974.

With the YF-16 programme underway, the incumbent SecDef, James R. Schlesinger, intimated that a production contract could possibly be forthcoming to the winner of the ADF contest, although the resultant aircraft would have to be available for the USAF, US Navy and foreign operators. Following on from this announcement came another in January 1975, from Air Force Secretary John McLucas, that the YF-16 had won the ACF contest. This in turn led to a contract for the FSD aircraft.

Production of the F-16 FSD aircraft, complete with changes from the earlier YF-16s, continued smoothly. Thus the first single-seater was ready for its maiden flight on 8 December 1976, with GD test pilot Neil Anderson at the controls. The first two-seater followed soon after, in this case both Anderson and Oestricher were aboard. First deliveries were made to the 388th TFW at Hill

AFB in January 1979, although the first pilots to use the F-16 in action were not from the USAF.

Israel takes the F-16 into combat

The first nation to use the F-16 in combat was Israel, whose air force first took the type to war on 7 June 1981, after only 14 months of service. The target was the nuclear reactor under construction at Osirak, near Baghdad, which was scheduled to come on line later that year. The strike was justified on the basis that Israeli intelligence sources were postulating that if the reactor was allowed to go critical then production of weapons grade plutonium would follow soon after. As Israel pursues a policy of protecting its borders and people at all costs, it is hardly surprising that the decision was quickly taken to attack and destroy the reactor buildings before they were completed.

The timing of the attack was critical, the raid had to be carried out before the radioactive rods were installed, otherwise there was a serious danger of lethal dust being released into the atmosphere. The aircraft for the mission were also carefully chosen. Top cover for the raid was to be provided by six F-15 Eagles, while the bomber aircraft would be F-16s. The choice of the latter was dependent upon its long range, the ground mapping mode built into its APG-66 radar and the accuracy of its navigation and attack systems.

Above: Eleven missile launch symbols are painted on the nose of 91-0402. All indicate successful launches against ground radar targets.

Right: F-16C 85-1444, was assigned to Major Ed Kinney during 1995 who, with his crew chief, appears to like the use of ducks to denote weapons launches in hostile environments. *(both Bob Archer/BBA Archive)*

The departure point for the raid, by now named Operation *Babylon*, although it was also referred to as *Opera*, was Etzion AB near Eilat in the south of Israel. As this would be a long mission in both time and distance, all 14 aircraft were fitted with external fuel tanks and aerial refuelling was carried out to top up the tanks. The route chosen took the formation over the tip of southern Jordan, followed by an incursion into Saudi Arabian airspace. Although not confirmed, it is postulated that the crews retuned their radios to frequencies used by the RJAF. Speaking Arabic and using RJAF callsigns, the formation pretended to be a Jordanian unit on a training flight. To deceive the Saudi air defence operation, the formation dropped below radar detection height to continue its progress undetected. Streaking low across the desert, the formation crossed the Iraqi border at high speed and low level, where it was fired upon by anti-aircraft artillery (AAA) units. Given the height and speed of the aircraft, the AAA units were unsuccessful and all aircraft passed undamaged.

The time over target was set for 06.30 that Sunday morning, since the French technicians working on the construction of the reactor were thought to be on a day off. Except for the border AAA reaction, the element of surprise was complete as the formation came in from the west. There was a smattering of AAA fire, but no surface-to-air missiles (SAMs) were fired, and no air defence fighters were launched. The F-16s attacked in two distinct waves, aiming primarily at the 32-m (105-ft) concrete cupola destined to cover the reactor material. The overall time needed to complete the entire raid was less than two minutes, using 2,000-lb (907-kg) bombs, deployed two per aircraft.

This shark-mouthed 74th FS F-16C is loaded with LANTIRN pods, a centreline ECM pod and practice bombs underwing. *(C P Russell Smith Collection)*

The debrief by the raid commander, Lt-Col Ze'ev Raz, was thorough, extensive and in some areas dramatic: 'We were briefed to fly a course over Eilat and Aqaba, and then south of Jordan along the Saudi Arabia border. The route is planned to avoid Arab villages and cities where we might be discovered, so we will fly over the desert area until we reach Baghdad. This is not the shortest route to fly, but it would avoid radar detection, so we will remain undetected just until we reach the target. On the way to the target we will fly at an altitude of 150 ft [46 m]. On our way back we will fly at high altitude so that refuelling can be carried out. Combat is to be avoided at all costs as the fuel margin leaves no room for error.

'About 20 km [12 miles] to the east of the reactor we will light the afterburner and start to climb. At the selected height we will bank over, identify the target and dive at a speed of 600 kt [1112 km/h; 691 mph] at an angle of 35°. Bombs release is set at an altitude of 3,500 ft [1067 m], aiming at the base of the structure. All pilots will drop their bombs at intervals of 5 seconds, it is estimated that eight will do the job, but to ensure success all 16 must hit the target, especially as the reactor is surrounded by high earth ramparts. Although it is possible that the

An F-16C from the 363rd FW based at Shaw AFB prepares to land after a practice attack sortie. With gear down and airbrakes extended, this Fighting Falcon is lightly loaded with just an ACMI pod on the right wing tip, underwing fuel tanks and practice bomb TERs on the wing centre pylons. *(Bob Archer/BBA Archive)*

formation could be attacked by AAA defences on the way to the target, all pilots must be aware that the reactor site has its own air defence system.'

The result of the raid was that the protective dome totally collapsed and that the surrounding buildings had been reduced to rubble. Unfortunately, one of the bombs hit a development laboratory, where it killed a French engineer working inside. Upon departure, the IDF/AF formation transited the way it had come in, passing through Arab airspace without interception or detection, before re-entering Israel to make a safe landing. American reaction to the raid was very condemning in public, although in private the Reagan administration was glad that the threat of an unstable nuclear power in the Middle East had been removed.

Further Israeli F-16 attacks

One of the tangible results of the American public disapproval was a delay in Fighting Falcon deliveries, although much speculation surrounds the fact that this batch was suffering component delays. This notwithstanding, the IDF/AF continued to use the F-16 for offensive purposes, one such raid being the attack upon Palestinian bases in Lebanon that began on

17 July 1981. Further raids were carried out during the early months of 1982, mainly over the Beka'a Valley in the Lebanon. During these encounters, the Syrian Arab Air Force (SAAF) put up a strong aerial resistance in the form of the MiG-23 'Flogger'. In combat the IDF/AF downed 92 enemy fighters, with the F-16 becoming the top MiG killer with 44 Syrian aircraft downed.

After these missions had been completed, a senior IDF/AF officer explained the high kill rate. It would appear that the SAAF, flying MiG-21, MiG-23 and Su-22 'Fitter' aircraft was inadequately briefed and trained in air combat tactics, thus it was a fairly easy task to shoot the Syrians down, although they did fire missiles and guns at their attackers.

On 28 April 1981 there was heightened tension with Syria which had begun to send ground forces and helicopters into the Jebel Snin area. That morning, further intelligence reports came in concerning the movement of Syrian transport helicopters into the area. The squadron commander and Major R, who was then a young lieutenant, were on interception readiness duty: 'At 09:00 we suddenly heard an ear-splitting siren wail. We ran to our planes, carried out a rapid start and took off. We flew over the sea at low

The F-16CJ Block 50/52 is the only version dedicated to carrying the AGM-88 HARM. The weapon can detect and destroy a target by homing in on its radar emissions. The F-16CJ's mission is to fly with other aircraft and attack the SAM sites that target them. This aircraft was part of the 79th FS of the 363rd FT based at Shaw AFB and wears an enlarged leaping tiger on its fin. (USAF)

altitude, west of Beirut. When we were right over the city we pulled upward to a patrol altitude of 20,000 ft [6096 m]. The squadron commander experienced a radar malfunction, and I thus became the lead plane, since I was supplying all of the data. We passed close by Riak airfield in the Lebanese Beka'a Valley. We descended to a lower altitude and divided the work between us, the squadron commander was in charge of communications with the control tower, and I relayed the data to him.

'My radar picked up a distant target. I locked onto it and we flew in its direction. I waited for permission to shoot, but it was slow in coming and I was finding it hard to maintain the missile lock. Then the missile lock disappeared. By now, with no missile lock, no permission to shoot and no permission to enter the area, we turned and headed towards a point to the south and west of Beirut. As we turned I picked up a target on the radar again.

'The target was moving 10 miles [16 km] north of Riak airfield, towards Jebel Snin. At long last we received permission to enter the area and permission to shoot. We flew at low altitude, at Mach 0.9, in the target's direction. I noticed that the lock wasn't very stable. There wasn't that much time left for thinking because we were nearing the minimum range for missile launch. I wasn't sure that it was a good launch although I fired anyway. Unfortunately the lock failed completely and the missile hit a hut on the ground.

'By now I could see the target clearly. It was a Syrian helicopter, which was later identified as an Mi-8. I passed over him, pulled up at a very high speed and tried to prepare for a second missile launch. The squadron commander overtook me and I suddenly noticed he was using his cannon to strafe the helicopter. I hadn't even thought of using the cannon until that point. The Syrian pilot executed a turn, meanwhile, and I saw the bursts of cannon fire shooting up the dirt just behind him.

'I was flying at 12,000 ft [3658 m] when the controller suddenly told us to break off contact and fly westward. I switched to cannon and went for the helicopter again, in a dive run. The controller intervened again and demanded we break off contact immediately. It turned out there was a group of unfriendly MiGs about 25 km [16 miles] east of us. I told the controller "immediately" and dived onto the helicopter at a speed of 570 kt [1056 km/h; 656 mph] from west to east, and pulled up behind him. It was flying about 10 m [33 ft] above the ground and I put my sights on his tail and opened fire.

'I fired a long burst, at the end of which a giant flame burst from the helicopter, which crashed to the ground and fell apart, billowing heavy smoke. The controller instructed us to disengage, again, and I informed him of the kill. I executed a very sharp turn westward, about an 8-*g* turn, and the squadron commander said on the radio: "very nice, Two".

'We climbed to higher altitude and flew homewards. We did a tight buzz over the base. Virtually the entire base was waiting for us on the ground. They'd been waiting for a victory for a long time. Everyone looked at the wing that had a missile missing and at the black soot that

the cannon bursts had left behind. They lifted me up on their shoulders, stood around me in a circle and bombarded me with questions. It was a great occasion, no doubt about it. And let's not forget, the unspoken rivalry with the F-15 squadrons also played a part in our pride.

'That same day another Mi-8 was shot down by the squadron's deputy commander. The following day, the Syrians advanced SAMs into the Beka'a, a move which was one of the factors that brought about the start of the Lebanon War.'

Three months after Major R's aerial victory, on 4 July 1981, Israeli F-16s encountered Syrian MiG-21s. It was Bastille Day, 14 years to the day since the Mirages' first aerial victory, against a MiG-21, and this time it was a Colonel A, flying an F-16, who shot down a MiG-21.

Col A: 'Our Skyhawks had attacked designated targets that day, and the Syrians tried to interfere, as they always did. When the attacks were over, my fuel supply was below the recommended minimum. I reported this to the controller and turned south, and the other formation continued the patrol.

'Over the Mediterranean, near Tyre, the

Equipped for a CAP, this F-16C hails from the 8th FW, better known as the famous 'Wolf Pack', whose badge features prominently on the fin. Famed for its exploits while flying Phantoms in Vietnam, the Wing currently resides at Kunsan AB, Korea. *(USAF)*

Captured on film at high altitude, this Shaw-based F-16C is a late-batch Block 40 aircraft that carries its ECM equipment externally, as evidenced by the pod on the centreline pylon. *(USAF)*

controller suddenly announced the presence of further MiGs. The second formation turned to meet them. A quick glance at the fuel gauge showed I was at the minimum, but still had just enough, therefore I turned back, heading north east. The radar registered a small green blip moving westward at speed before the target turned south in my direction, although I suspected that he was heading home. The range between us decreased. Even though I didn't have eye contact with the MiG, the lock remained steady. I identified a dark green MiG. The familiar buzzing sound told me that the missile had acquired its target. I was at ideal range. A press on the button was followed by the sound of the missile launch. Then there was a tremendous explosion and a fireball slammed into the hill ahead.'

US combat

Although the IDF/AF was seeing combat with its Fighting Falcons, it was not until the Gulf War of 1991 that USAF F-16s experienced combat action. When the forces of Iraq invaded the territory of Kuwait in August 1990, Saddam Hussein had misjudged the reaction of the western nations. A Coalition of many forces was quickly assembled to reinforce those of Saudi Arabia. Some of the first aircraft deployed to the Middle East were the F-16s of the USAF. Eventually some 249 of the type would be in theatre, ranging from the earliest F-16As to be employed on air defence duties, to the latest F-16C/Ds, that were destined to act in the ground attack role. Given that the Iraqi air force (IAF) displayed a marked reluctance to venture towards the Saudi border, it should come as no surprise that no shoot-downs were scored by the USAF's F-16s. In fact, much of the IAF strength ended up in the hands of Iraq's mortal enemy, Iran.

The lack of aerial combat meant that the F-16s were fully engaged in attacking ground targets, finally achieving a total of 13,480 sorties, some 4,000 being flown at night. Each of these flights averaged just over three hours and involved an aerial refuelling. One vital item missing from the F-16's inventory was the LANTIRN pod, which had only just completed its development trials. The small number in theatre was allocated to the F-15E Eagles to improve their targeting accuracy.

The lack of a specialist targeting system meant that the F-16s were forced to bomb using their on-board continuously-computed impact point (CCIP) system. Although the little jet was more than capable of achieving a circular-error probability (CEP) of 9 m (30 ft) under normal circumstances, the varied threats posed by AAA and SAMs soon changed that to at least 61 m (200 ft). Allied to the altitude increase when bombing attacks moved to medium altitudes, were attempts at various times to deliver dumb bombs at supersonic speeds, a technique that had not been fully tested.

Possibly the biggest air raid involving the F-16 was assembled on 19 January 1991. The formation consisted of F-4G Phantoms for SEAD (suppression of enemy air defences), EF-111s for jamming purposes, F-15 Eagles for CAP (combat air patrol) and 64 Fighting Falcons drawn from all the units in theatre. The intended target was downtown Baghdad and the first package arrived overhead and bombed through the cloud cover, the suppression aircraft continuing their vital task. Unfortunately for the final wave the weather cleared and two F-16s were hit. Although they struggled to reach safe territory, both pilots were forced to eject to be recovered some time later. A further, similar, attack was undertaken against Osirak, although this time the Iraqi forces were waiting and ignited smoke pots to conceal the target.

In addition to regular bombing missions, the F-16s also found themselves being used in the fast FAC (forward air control) role. Working a set area, each F-16 would confirm targets nominated by ground forces, before calling in an air strike. Another role allocated to the Falcons was that of battlefield air interdiction (BAI), during which they managed to destroy at least 360 armoured vehicles, while also finding time to destroy 'Scud' sites pinpointed by orbiting J-STARS (Joint Surveillance Target Attack Radar System) aircraft. Overall losses for the USAF F-16 fleet during *Desert Storm* totalled three, two during combat and another caused by a fuel leak.

Northern and Southern Watch

With the conclusion of *Desert Storm*, the F-16s that remained in theatre were allocated to Operations *Northern* and *Southern Watch*, which had created rigidly enforced no-fly zones at the north and south of Iraq. It was during one of these patrols that a USAF F-16 finally achieved an air-to-air kill. On 27 December 1992, while F-16s were patrolling in the southern part of Iraq, the Iraqis despatched a MiG-25 to test the no-fly zone. Detecting the MiG, the F-16s launched their AMRAAMs, in the first combat use of this missile, and scored a confirmed shoot down. On 17 January 1993, the patrollers policing *Northern Watch* had their turn for aerial success when they shot down two MiGs, types unconfirmed, before returning to their base at Incirlik AB, Turkey.

Operation Deny Flight

Once the no-fly zones had been established, the USAF deployed further combat-ready F-16s to patrol above the war torn skies of the former Yugoslavia. Code named *Deny Flight*, the operation covered the Bosnia-Herzegovina region and was intended to control Serbian aggression against their weaker neighbours. The Serbian air force decided to test the resolve of the patrolling fighters on 28 February 1994, when a flight of Jastreb light attack aircraft bombed a factory in Bosnia. Airborne above them was a pair of F-16s from the 86th FW. Given permission to open fire, the fighters launched AIM-120 missiles, that destroyed one intruder, before descending to a lower level to engage the rest with AIM-9 Sidewinders. In the ensuing fracas, a further two Jastrebs were despatched, while another pair was destroyed by other aircraft from the same FW.

Operational intensity increased in 1995, when ground attack missions were added to the F-16's lexicon. By this time the LANTIRN pods were fully cleared for service, so the aircraft of the 31st FW, based at Aviano AB, Italy, began intensive training to use them. The outcome of this surge in activity was the launch of a strike against a

Serbian ammunition dump near Pale, during May 1995. The LGBs dropped scored direct hits. Following on from this initial sortie, a series of intensive strikes, code named Operation *Deliberate Force*, began against Serbian positions in August 1995. During this period some 300 LGBs were dropped on designated targets, with a 90 per cent success rate and no observed collateral damage. As all the missions were being flown at medium altitudes, only one of the two LANTIRN pods was installed, the terrain-following radar (TFR) pod being left behind to reduce the F-16's drag coefficient.

To achieve the best results from the LANTIRN system, data was fed in by GPS to the onboard avionics. This in turn aimed the pod's IR imager towards a target being painted by another remote source. As well as designating targets, the IR system could also record the strike using onboard video which could determine the accuracy of the attack.

Operations over Bosnia were not without consequences, as Captain Scott O'Grady found out when his F-16 was shot out from underneath him by an SA-6 missile in June 1995. Escaping the initial attempts of ground troops to capture him, Scott O'Grady was rescued six days later by a helicopter supported

As the furthest F-16A peels off to intercept a possible bogey, the pilot of the nearest aircraft looks on. Both aircraft come from the South Dakota ANG, better known as the 'Happy Hooligans'. *(USAF)*

by a force of F/A-18s armed with HARMs (High-Speed Anti-Radar Missiles).

Once Operation *Deliberate Force* was fully underway, the Aviano-based Fighting Falcons were joined by those of Spangdahlem AB, Germany. Unlike the Italy-based aircraft, which were Block 40 machines, the newcomers were to Block 50 standard, which allowed them to carry the full range of missiles and bombs already cleared for the F-16, as well as anti-radar equipment. Carrying the ASQ-213 HARM targeting system (HTS), plus the AGM-88 HARMs themselves, this group of F-16s added an extra bite to operations over Bosnia. Acting in the Wild Weasel defence suppression role, the F-16s fired nine HARMs that were credited with putting their targets off air. Although the USAF is very wary about accuracy figures concerning this weapon, it is thought that it has a greater than 90 per cent success rate. With the uprated Fighting Falcons operating within an attack formation, the chances of attack by SAMs was drastically reduced.

Following on from their success during *Desert Storm*, the Aviano based F-16s were employed in the fast-FAC role, although this time it had been renamed Airborne Forward Air Control (AFAC). Target marking was carried out using the venerable 'Willie Pete' phosphorus target-marking rocket, with results being supported by the Sure Strike data link system. The premise behind these sorties is that the AFAC aircraft

overflies the designated battle zone, while remaining in contact with both air and ground forces. When ground troops required support, the incoming F-16s would arrive over the target able to identify their targets quickly, either by the drifting smoke from the 'Willie Petes', a laser target designator, or the Sure Strike data link.

Operation *Allied Force*

The situation within Yugoslavia, although volatile, had remained relatively stable, however, this all changed when Serbian forces began ethnic cleansing against Albanians within Kosovo during late 1998. In response, NATO and the European Union responded strongly, in a move that many had called for over the years. Under the title Operation *Allied Force*, deployments of extra aircraft were approved by President Clinton, based upon the recommendations of SecDef Cohen. Operations began against targets within Serbia on 24 March 1999, when land, and sea-based aircraft, became fully involved.

Numerically, the F-16 was the most important aircraft employed within *Allied Force*. Not only were USAF aircraft involved, but other NATO F-16s also undertook combat missions. During the first day of airborne attacks, targets in Serbia, Kosovo and Montenegro were hit. On day two of the campaign, 25 March, air-to-air combat was joined with Serbian MiG-29s. One of the victors was a Dutch F-16, J-063, of No. 322 Sqdn, while the other kills went to USAF F-15.

During the 80 days of the air campaign, F-16s were deployed from various countries within the NATO framework. The USAF deployed the largest number of aircraft. The majority was based at Aviano AB, Italy. There were 58 Fighting Falcons of the CG and CJ varieties at Aviano. Further north, at Bandirma AB, in Turkey, another twelve F-16CJs were ensconced. From Belgium came a dozen F-16As which were based at Amendola, Italy. The RDAF sent eight machines to Grazzanise, also in Italy. A slightly smaller, but no less effective force, was supplied by Norway, which sent six aircraft to join the Danish force at Grazzanise. Outside of the USAF detachment, the KLu sent the largest F-16 force, to liaise with the Belgians in Italy, where twenty aircraft landed to join the force.

Operation *Enduring Freedom*

On 11 September 2001, the world changed for ever when hijacked airliners slammed into the twin towers of the World Trade Center in New York, and the Pentagon building in Washington, DC. Resisting the immediate desire to lash out indiscriminately, the US created a measured response to the attack. Intelligence sources had placed the blame squarely at the feet of the Saudi Arabian-born terrorist Osama Bin Laden. Further investigations placed the terrorist chief in hiding inside Taliban-controlled Afghanistan. Placing not only Afghanistan, but other nations suspected of supporting terrorism under warning, the US began the preparations for retaliatory strikes that would be known as Operation *Enduring Freedom*. Although diplomatic means were initially used in an attempt to extract Bin Laden from Afghanistan, the Taliban remained steadfastly defiant. Much of the subsequent aerial warfare was carried out using long-range bombers and carrier-based aircraft. The role of the F-16 within the US is currently aimed at preparing crews for overseas service and providing air defence over those locations that were deemed vulnerable to further attack under the code name Operation *Noble Eagle*.

Outside of America a dozen F-16CJs have been deployed as part of the 366th Air Expeditionary Wing, based 'somewhere in the Middle East', possibly Bahrain, a location that has been used before by Air Combat Command. Although the version of the F-16 flown by the 366th is aimed at defence suppression, its aircraft scored a couple of noticeable firsts while taking part in *Enduring Freedom*. New weapons were deployed by the 389th Expeditionary Fighter Squadron (EFS), also known as the 'T-Bolts'. The first was the GBU-31 Joint Direct Attack Munition (JDAM), which uses a special tail kit that reads GPS

43

co-ordinates to steer 2,000-lb (907-kg) bombs to their targets through any kind of weather, with an accuracy of 43 ft (13 m) or less.

The honour of using this weapon in combat fell to Col Bill Andrews, commander of the 366th Air Expeditionary Group, and Captain Paul Kirmis, a pilot with the 389th EFS, who had their names written into the history books when their F-16s dropped JDAMs on Afghanistan on 29 November 2001.

Another new weapon deployed in Afghanistan was the CBU-103 cluster bomb which, in common with the GBU-31, is capable of being used in all weather conditions. Captains Mark Piper and Mark Wisher of the 389th EFS recorded F-16 firsts when they dropped CBU-103 Wind-Corrected Munitions Dispensers on 13 November 2001.

Training for the use of CBU-103s and GBU-31s had started in 2001 prior to the events of 11 September, at training ranges for Mountain Home AFB, Idaho, and included 'train-as-we-fight' scenarios with different threat aircraft and simulated SAMs.

Operation *Noble Eagle*, the heightened air defence effort over the continental USA put in force since 11 September 2001, relies on the F-15 and F-16. Here a 177th FW F-16C of the New Jersey ANG plays its part. *(USAF)*

Only one other country has used the F-16 in anger, this being Pakistan, although very little information has been forthcoming concerning the use of the Fighting Falcon in PAF service.

Other roles

Outside of the more warlike roles thrust upon it, the F-16 Fighting Falcon has been employed in the development of various aspects of aerodynamic and engine behaviour. One of the prime sponsors of these experiments has been NASA, which has pursued this goal in concert with the US armed forces at both the NASA Dryden Flight Research Center and the facilities at Edwards AFB. The first use of an F-16 by NASA was of the XL version, which made its first flight under its new management on 3 May 1990. It initially investigated active and passive methods of reducing turbulence. It was some years later when the two-seat F-16XL joined the programme, making its appearance on 13 October 1995, although it was more modified than the single-seater. Pilots involved with the F-16XL and AFTI versions include Stephen Ishmael as Chief Project Pilot, with James Smolka as project pilot for F-16 AFTI; while Dana Purifoy was project pilot for F-16 AFTI and F-16XL; Roger Smith was project pilot for F-16 AFTI and William Dana was project pilot for F-16 AFTI.

4. Accomplishments

For any aircraft to achieve a measure of fame is a great accomplishment, but to do so against the odds is even more remarkable. Therefore the widespread acceptance of the Lockheed Martin / General Dynamics F-16 Fighting Falcon, not only into the ranks of the USAF, but also on the world stage, is quite stunning.

To understand the success of the F-16 it is necessary to place it in a historical context. When the idea of a lightweight fighter was first mooted, the USAF and aircraft manufacturers were embroiled in the pursuit of just one goal: speed. To gain a production contract, a new fighter had to be capable of reaching at least Mach 1 and preferably Mach 2. Range, weaponry and manoeuvrability were of little importance compared with speed.

Following this goal led to the development of the Century Series of fighters: fast, complicated, initially unreliable and, as later events would show, lightly armed. Then the Vietnam War happened and gaps in the USAF inventory became apparent. The greatest and most telling of these was the lack of aircraft dedicated to bombing and ground attack missions. To counteract this deficiency, some Century series fighters, in particular the F-100, had their structures strengthened, hardpoints added and their avionics upgraded. The F-100 joined the F-105 Thunderchief in attack missions over Vietnam. Overall, however, the changes to the F-100 failed to vastly improve its survival rate,

and both types proved vulnerable to all forms of ground fire, which could render their closely packed and complicated systems useless. In the event it was mostly the bravery of the crews that made them a success.

In contrast there were alternatives that were successful and both would be influential in the development of the F-16. The first was the little-noticed and lightly-regarded A-37 Dragonfly, which would gain an outstanding reputation, especially among FACs and troops in contact. To achieve this reputation the little Cessna had a number of attributes. These included a good thrust-to-weight ratio, accurate weapons delivery and the ability to tote a heavy ordnance load for its size.

The second machine that had an influence on the F-16 was the doyen of lightweight fighters, the Northrop F-5 Freedom Fighter. In contrast to the heavyweights in the USAF inventory, the F-5 had no sophisticated radar, relying mainly upon a ranging radar for target acquisition, and the ability to economically carry a reasonable weapons load at speed. The Northrop aircraft repaid the faith of its designers during an operational test deployment to Vietnam. Although it never entered front-line service with the USAF, it did become an export success with the world's air forces.

It was against this background of conflict that the ADF/LWF concept was born, courtesy of a Pentagon weapons specialist and a cadre of disillusioned combat pilots who thought that spending vast amounts of taxpayers' dollars on aircraft complete with extraneous bells and whistles, was an expensive waste. To support their arguments they produced evidence that many of the hi-tech innovations incorporated into these new, expensive, machines were ineffective and unreliable. Eventually their persistence would pay off, when the first YF-16 proof-of-concept aircraft made its first flight on 2 February 1974. From that point the Fighting Falcon developed into the multi-role machine that is the mainstay of the world's air forces today.

Low-cost airframe

Underpinning the whole ethos of the F-16 is its airframe structure, which is manufactured mainly from aluminium alloy to keep build costs down. The design engineers at General Dynamics, Fort Worth strived to create an airframe that was modular in construction, fairly simple to assemble and avoided the use of sophisticated constructional techniques that would cause problems later, should repair become necessary. As well as the 80 per cent aluminium alloy in its airframe, the F-16 features 8 per cent steel in areas of high stress, 1.5 per cent titanium in high heat areas and 3 per cent composite materials. To further keep manufacturing costs down much of the airframe is made from sheet metal, with chemically etched components being kept to no more than 2 per cent.

In contrast, the actual design is very hi-tech, since the latest technology was employed to plan the complete structure. Using the twin theories of wing/body blending and relaxed structure stability, the GD engineering team managed to create an airframe that is some 590 kg (1,300 lb) lighter than would have been the outcome using more conventional design techniques. To emphasise the point to the Pentagon, possibly not a good idea given their previous track record with the F-111 cost overruns, the GD engineers theorised that the whole airframe would cost approximately $60 per lb, which reduced the airframe cost by some $80,000. Often, as an

aircraft design continues, the overall weight grows. However, learning lessons from problems with the earlier General Dynamics F-111, also a Fort Worth product, the GD designers exercised rigorous control over F-16 airframe weight, so that by January 1978, after nearly three years' of continued development, the entire aircraft's weight had risen by no more than 5 per cent. Thus, the F-16, which had started at 10060 kg (22,179 lb), had only increased to 10595 kg (23,357 lb). Much of this extra weight was accounted for by increased operational capability modifications and other changes aimed at improving maintenance procedures.

To prove the structural viability of the F-16, the fifth development airframe was encased in a test rig that incorporated at least 100 hydraulically-driven rams. These simulated the various loads experienced during take-off, landing and combat manoeuvring up to loads of 10 g. When the summer of 1978 was reached, this airframe had flown 16,000 simulated hours in a controlled manner. As the simulation continued some cracks did develop in certain highly loaded bulkheads, these requiring redesign for aircraft under construction. Those already in service were submitted to a modification programme.

To give the F-16 its structural strength and to allow it to pull the high g loads generated by combat manoeuvring, all of the minor sub-assemblies are built up into major sub-assemblies consisting of the forward fuselage, including the cockpit; the centre fuselage, including the wing attachment points; and the rear fuselage. Although the fuselage is an excellent example of the aerodynamic blender's art, the bones beneath it are conventional longerons, frames and stringers, with the production assembly breaks located just aft of the cockpit and just forward of the fin. A further advantage gained using this method of assembly is that extra fuel can be carried; an estimated 31 per cent more than in a more conventional airframe.

The aerodynamics of the F-16 are a revelation owing to the extensive blending between the wing and fuselage, which is practised around all three axes. Such is the subtlety of this process that there is no defined join between the fuselage and the wings, this being further reinforced by the leading edge strakes. These extensions not only continue the blending theme, but they also improve handling at high AoA by generating vortices that maintain the energy of the boundary layer over the wing; this in turn delays stalling of the inner wing section and retains directional stability. A further bonus gained from these strakes is that the main wing area can be reduced, as can overall weight.

Another advantage of the F-16's small airframe is that the avionics, fuel and other systems are concentrated close to the centre of gravity. A similarly equipped conventional airframe would be about 1.5 m (5 ft) longer and some 249 kg (550 lb) heavier.

Wing design

The wing increases in thickness towards the root. Its structural strength and torsional stiffness are maintained by the use of five spars and eleven ribs, the whole being covered, top and bottom, by a single skin that has reinforced cut-outs for system access. To further reduce the size and weight of the wing and to improve manoeuvrability the wing has leading edge manoeuvring flaps while the trailing edge has flaperons which also assist in handling throughout the envelope.

Whether the engineers at Fort Worth realised it or not, they had created a powerful lifting body, since in 'clean' configuration, the whole aircraft generates lift. Although this is not ideal for supersonic performance, it does improve the behaviour of the F-16 at high AoA. Assisting the

This close-up of the nose gear of an F-16 reveals a wealth of detail. The pin (with red tag attached) is that for the downlock, while the small open panel houses the armament safety break. To tow the F-16 safely on the ground, the torque link pin needs to be removed, allowing the nosewheel to castor freely. Also worthy of note is the anti-erosion paint applied to the front of the centreline fuel tank. *(Jens Jensen)*

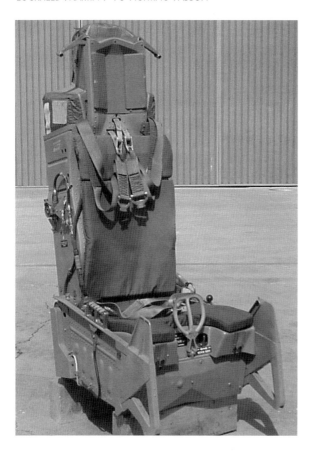

This three-quarter view of an ACES II shows the location of the ejection seat separation handles plus the positioning of the straps. *(USAF)*

F-16 to perform within its flight envelope are leading-edge manoeuvring flaps and trailing-edge flaperons, both of which are capable of deflecting throughout their full ranges at 35°/s. To ensure that there is no overstress of the airframe the tailplanes are integrated, via the flight control system, with both sets of flaps, controlling the speed of flap movement. The ability of the FCS (Flight Control System) to translate the pilot's inputs into manoeuvres almost instantly, allows the F-16 to out-turn most aircraft and gives it the ability to jink at high speed and low level to avoid hostile defences. There was a downside to this clever design, however, since problems occurred with the leading edge flap actuators, which had been engineered to fit into a space no more than 3.8 cm (1.5 in) deep. During a maintenance inspection, signs of wear were found in the actuator and drive train. The initial fix was to replace any defective actuators while a more permanent modification was engineered. This has since been embodied.

Tail structure

The fin is of a similar construction to the wing, being multi-sparred and ribbed throughout. Externally the fin is skinned with a graphite epoxy, although its tip is made from aluminium alloy. The ventral fins are also manufactured from composite materials, although their mounting points are of an alloy material. Also located under the fuselage is the runway arrestor hook for use in emergencies.

The tailplanes of the early-build F-16s were replaced on the production line by items of increased size as part of MSIP Phase 1. Both versions are single-piece items, constructed in a similar manner to the wings and fin, with multiple spars and ribs and a graphite epoxy skin. Located inboard of the tailplanes are the split-type petal airbrakes. When selected to the open position, they extend to a maximum deflection of 60°. The new tailplanes were incorporated under Engineering Change Proposal ECP 425 and were required to cope with increased weapon loads.

Undercarriage

Supporting the greater bulk of the F-16 are the main undercarriage units, which retract forwards under single doors. At one stage it was planned that these doors would provide mounting points for such missiles as the AIM-7 Sparrow. Supporting the nose is a single-wheel nose undercarriage unit that is located aft of the intake. In this manner the engine is protected from FOD damage by debris thrown up by the nosewheel. The location of the intake also protects it from airflow disturbances caused by violent manoeuvres. Such is the complexity of the blending involved in creating the intake, that it is possible that at an AoA exceeding 25°, the mass airflow is actually entering the intake at an angle of 10°. To assist in keeping the overall unit cost and spare parts costs down, much of the F-16's components are interchangeable. This includes the tailplanes, flaperons, many of the actuators and 80 per cent of the undercarriage components.

Cockpit

At the heart of the F-16 sits the pilot in a cockpit which represented a great departure from conventional cockpit design. One of the most obvious diversions is the angle at which the ejection seat is installed. Numerous reasons have been given for the 30° installation of the seat. One is that it allowed a smaller pilot to fly the aircraft, another is that at such an angle the pilot was capable of withstanding higher g forces. Some calculations put this at 9 g. The seat is an ACES II (Advanced Concept Ejection Seat) unit offering zero/zero capability and incorporating an emergency oxygen supply, a liferaft and a URT-33C radio beacon. The seat's motive power is provided by a rocket pack augmented by a small vernier rocket motor which is stabilised by a pitch rate gyro. Following on from the realignment of the seat, the General Dynamics design team decided to delete the conventional control column and replace it with a side-stick controller located on the right hand side console. Initially the relocated stick had no actual movement, gaining its inputs from sensors in the base. However, experience during the development phase showed that pilots felt happier if there was some movement built into the system. Located at various points around the controller are numerous buttons and switches. These, combined with similar protrusions on the throttle, give the F-16 true Hands On Throttle And Stick (HOTAS) capability.

Above the cockpit is a canopy that gives remarkable all-round vision. Except for a small fairing to the rear, the greater part of the canopy is a single item that hinges behind the pilot. To reduce radar signature and to stop the whole cockpit becoming a greenhouse, the canopy has a reflective gold layer in its make up, this also assists in cutting down glare on the instrument panel. The first examples, although designed to withstand the strike of a 4-lb (1.8-kg) bird at 350 kt (649 km/h; 403 mph), failed to withstand the impact adequately. Two redesigns later and a heavier, more resilient, assembly was fitted as standard on the production line. As well as having a heavier canopy frame, the new item's polycarbonate is 1.3 cm (0.5 in) thick and is curved in such a way as to reduce optical distortion to the minimum. Thanks to this canopy, the F-16 pilot enjoys a full 360° all-round vision in the horizontal plane, while the view over the nose is 15° below the horizontal plane. The sideways view extends downward some 40°.

MSIP

Advances in technology led to the implementation of the Multinational Staged Improvement Program which was initiated in February 1981, as part of Engineering Change Proposal ECP 350. The modifications included structural strengthening to provide for the AIM-120 AMRAAM and hardpoint mountings on the lower intake sides for the LANTIRN system. Strengthening of the wings allowed their centre pylons to be uprated to carry loads of 1588 kg (3,500 lb). Also incorporated during MSIP 1 were mountings for an onboard ECM system. In the event, however, this was not installed in its intended form.

Powerplant

When the F-X fighter finally evolved into the McDonnell Douglas F-15 Eagle, its engine was spun off into the F-16 programme. Development of the Pratt & Whitney F100 turbofan began in August 1968. Unlike other engines of the period this new powerplant, like its General Electric competitor, pushed available technology and metallurgy to their fullest limits. The nearest contender was the GE TF30 whose specific excess power was less than that required, while its weight was too great for the size of aircraft.

With its arrestor hook lowered to provide access, this F-16's engine is inspected by two civilian engineers. Note the plethora of panels that can be removed to allow inspection of the powerplant while it is still mounted in the airframe. (Lockheed Martin)

The task that faced Pratt & Whitney was to develop a lighter engine that could produce another 25 per cent higher thrust in comparison with available technology. Development proceeded apace and a few months later a demonstration engine emerged which was lighter in weight, had higher thrust and a comparatively low rate of fuel consumption in comparison with the TF30.

The F100 is an axial-flow turbofan with a bypass ratio of 0.7:1. Unlike earlier engines the F100 has two shafts, with one carrying a three-stage compressor which drives a two-stage turbine. The second shaft mounts a ten-stage compressor which drives another two-stage turbine. The engine is 485 cm (191 in) long with an external diameter of 88.4 cm (34.8 in) and a gross weight of 1392 kg (3,068 lb). As well as using multiple stages to improve the performance of its engine, Pratt & Whitney also evolved other new technologies, including powder metallurgy. This innovative technology uses powdered metal which is forced into moulds and formed into components. Not only does this improve the kinetic heat handling of each item, it also improves its fatigue life. This is in total contrast to the earlier methods of production which used casting and machining to manufacture each component. This method quite often created hidden stress points that could fail in use.

This advanced metal technology was put to good use, since the operating temperature of the F100 is far higher than that of earlier powerplants. These are rated at around 982°C (1,800°F), while the newer engine operates at temperatures in the region of 1400°C (2,552°F). During test-bench running, the thrust produced by the F100 without afterburner was in the 66.71-kN (15,000 lb st) class, while in full reheat 111.18 kN (25,000 lb st) was generated. In contrast, the F100-200s fitted to the F-16 are slightly restricted, thus, at normal dry rating the installed F100 generates 55.23 kN (12,420 lb st), while full Military Intermediate thrust is set at 65.24 kN (14,670 lb st). Fuel consumption at these ratings is 0.69 lb SFC (Specific Fuel Consumption) which is the amount of thrust produced for each pound of fuel burned per hour while at the higher output it rises to 0.71 SFC. In full afterburner, with the engine delivering 105.97 kN (23,830 lb st), the fuel consumption rises to 2.17 SFC. This equates to a burn rate of 390 kg (860 lb) per minute.

When the YF-16 first flew with the F100 engine, it seemed that they were a perfect match. This was in complete contrast to the F-15 Eagle experience, where problems with overspeed had been encountered due to inadequate engine/fuel cooling. The initial series of test flights continued without incident until one of the prototype F-16s experienced a stagnation stall. A further three

engine stalls occurred, all being at the full limits of the performance envelope. Further tweaks to the engine and the intake have virtually cured this problem, although all pilots are aware that such a problem may occur.

With the P&W F100 installed as the primary engine in the F-16, thought turned to installing other types of engine for countries not cleared for such advanced technology. The only such attempt saw the engine that powers the F-4 Phantom grafted into the F-16. Although the GE J79 had been a great servant in the past, it was at the end of its design life. Various features, including the J79's single drive shaft, meant that it was no longer capable of further development. Even so, at least one prototype, designated as the F-16/79, was test flown. However, results were disappointing in comparison with those of the F100-powered version. When the later engine was finally cleared for export, the J79-powered F-16 was killed off.

An alternative primary engine

One option that has seen further development, is the plan to find an alternative primary engine for the F-16. A potential engine candidate came out of a programme to find an alternative powerplant for the Grumman F-14 Tomcat. General Electric

In common with most aircraft, the F-16 appears cluttered when landing since the airbrakes and undercarriage cause discontinuous lines. Close observation of the undercarriage units in this shot reveals them to be in the relaxed position. On touch-down, the nose leg will compress, while both main units will splay slightly outward as they take the aircraft's weight. *(Damien Burke)*

was selected as the prime contractor to develop the engine that would later become known as the F101. The programme initially covered five development engines, known as the Derivative Fighter Engine (DFE), which cost the DoD $100 million. The first test-bench runs of the new engine took place on 30 December 1979. Once flight testing of the F101 had been completed, few changes were required to the F-16 airframe to accommodate it. The greatest of these was an intake assembly of enlarged size, since the F101 requires a larger air mass to operate efficiently. In addition, new-build F-16C/D airframes from Block 30/32 onwards have mountings for both types of engine, although they are not interchangeable in service. The F101 turbofan is now designated F110.

Avionics innovations

It is in the field of avionics, including cockpit display systems, that the F-16 has been, and continues to be, innovative. The aircraft is also interesting in terms of its FCS, since without its flight control computer the F-16 is virtually unflyable. In its earliest incarnation as the YF-16, the type's avionics suite was as simple as possible given that it was proposed only as an ADF. Once the two YF-16s had proved their ability to fly

This shot of a smartly turned out Norwegian F-16 shows quite clearly the shape of the increased-area tailplanes introduced early on in the Fighting Falcon production cycle. *(Bob Archer/BBA Archive)*

safely, the subsequent batch of F-16A/B FSD aircraft were modified to carry an avionics suite more suited to the combat scenarios of the late 1970s and early 1980s.

At the heart of the F-16 is the MIL-STD 1553 multiplex databus which allows the various computers and more importantly, their languages, to interface with each other. This reduces the need for the extensive cabling and interfaces previously required for the distribution of data and command signals. The lightweight digital switching interface was a cheaper and lighter alternative to cabling. It also allowed each systems manufacturer to use their own preferred programming language, safe in the knowledge that their equipment would work with fewer glitches than before.

As soon as the role of the F-16 in USAF service had been clarified, a radar system capable of multi-mode tasking was selected. This was the Westinghouse APG-66, featuring a planar-array scanner which was better at despatching and receiving Doppler signals than earlier antenna designs.

When the initial air-to-air mode tests on the APG-66 had been successfully completed, a request was for air-to-surface modes to be added. In order to keep development costs down a certain amount of compromise was undertaken in implementing these modes, especially in the area of the planar radar array. The greatest loss was in the quality of ground mapping from high

altitudes which is less than optimal; however, the F-16 spends much of its combat time at lower altitudes where this deficiency is less noticeable. Possibly the greatest exponent of the ground-mapping mode was the IDF/AF during its low level attack on the nuclear plant near Baghdad.

Within the spectrum of the I/J Bands in which the APG-66 operates are sixteen separate frequencies, of which four are selectable by the pilot at any one time. The weight of the whole system is 134 kg (296 lb) and it occupies a volume of 0.1 m^3 (3.6 cu ft), making it one of the most lightweight and space-efficient radar systems ever built. Further weight reductions, although minuscule, were achieved by transferring most of the controls to the throttle and side-stick controllers as part of the HOTAS arrangement. Also assisting the pilot in reducing the in-cockpit workload is the automatic range switching facility, which adjusts as the target moves.

The primary air-combat mode is look down, which provides a clutter-free display of detected targets. Fighter-size targets can be successfully discerned from all angles, including nose- and tail-on, out to a range of 30 nm (56 km; 35 miles). A similar performance is available in look-up mode, should the system detect a higher flying target. In total there are four air-to-air combat modes including range while scan, dogfight, designated and slewable. In contrast there are seven air-to-ground modes, which are centred about the radar's continuously computed release point (CCRP) facility.

As well as land mapping, the APG-66 system is also capable of sea searching using the Doppler principle. Sea Mode 1 employs a frequency-agile beam that is capable of operating in sea state 4 conditions, while Sea Mode 2 uses a narrower beam that can operate in higher sea states. Further features include a series of beacon navigation modes that can operate in conjunction with ground-based beacons, or an air-to-air mode that assists in the tracking of tankers for inflight refuelling.

Although the APG-66 radar was adequate for the initial roles assigned to the F-16, its

technology became dated. Therefore, with the advent of the F-16C/D Block 25, the system installed in the nose of the Fighting Falcon was replaced by the more advanced Hughes, later Northrop Grumman, APG-68 radar. Included in the new system was increased range capability, with better resolution and an increased number of modes. In order that the data be better presented to the pilot, a larger HUD was fitted. Support was also built in for the AGM-65 Maverick missile.

LANTIRN

Probably one of the most important upgrades applied to the F-16 was that which allowed compatibility with the LANTIRN system. On USAF aircraft LANTIRN is contained in two pods, one of which contains the laser targeting unit while the other houses the FLIR navigation system. On the F-16, the pods are mounted under the intake, one to each side of the nose undercarriage bay. Given their complexity both pods, manufactured by Lockheed Martin, are exceptionally small, the navigation pod being no more than 30.5 cm (12 in) in diameter with an overall length of 198 cm (78 in). Total weight is 195 kg (430 lb). Installed within the pod are a Ku-band terrain following radar (TFR), a wide-field-of-view FLIR and a computer and power supply. The radar, coupled to the computer, allows the F-16 to fly at high speed and low level and is capable of manoeuvring the aircraft 'hands off'. The FLIR has a field of view that encompasses 28° in azimuth and 21° in elevation, and its image can can be superimposed on the HUD. The system also gives the pilot excellent vision in darkness and in bad weather. The targeting pod, which is slightly larger in size, also contains a FLIR and a laser transmitter/receiver. All are protected by a stabilisation system that is able to compensate for vibration and manoeuvring. The centre section contains electronics and data processors and a boresight correlator. The latter passes target tracking and lock-on data to the aircraft's systems, which in turn update the air-to-ground weapons. Both

This Ohio ANG machine is parked on a flightline specifically designated for the F-16, since in front of the intake is a red-painted area that warns of the suction danger from the underslung intake. (C P Russell Smith Collection)

pods have their own environmental-control systems, reducing dependency upon the carrier aircraft. As each pod is a single entity it is possible for the F-16 to fly its missions with only one fitted, although commanders prefer their aircraft to have both available since most missions flown are of the 'pop up' variety, where the approach is made at low level before climbing for weapons release.

In the cockpit

In the F-16's cockpit, many of the old familiar gauges have been replaced by electronic displays, with much vital data being displayed on the HUD. The main 'glass' displays are concerned with systems and weapons management, although they can also display navigation data in 'heads-down' mode. The HUD, manufactured by Pilkington in the UK, also acts as a reinforced screen which protects the occupant should the canopy be penetrated by a projectile, or be jettisoned.

In the fields of communications and electronic jamming the F-16 systems designers made great strides. From the outset, their intention was to keep the number of communications aerials to a minimum n order to reduce the aircraft's drag coefficient. Nevertheless, located at various points about the airframe are aerials for the TACAN (Tactical Air Navigation system), VHF (very high frequency), glide slope localiser, UHF (ultra high frequency) and IFF systems, plus sensors for the detection of hostile radar transmissions.

Positive protection of the F-16 in hostile skies comes courtesy of active ECM, which has been a feature of the type since its earliest service days. The external evidence of an ECM system is often an ALQ-131 pod on the aircraft's centreline pylon, however, current-build machines have the AN/ALQ-178 internal ECM system fitted and the centreline pylon is more often seen carrying other stores. Turkish F-16s have the RAPPORT III internal ECM system installed.

Up to the era that spawned the F-16 and its rivals, all aircraft used a mechanical or electro-mechanical system of flight control. When General Dynamics approached the F-16 design, one of the first decisions made was to use a computer-controlled flight system complete with FBW. Using FBW, the aircraft could be made smaller and the control system installation lighter. Another advantage of such a system is the almost instant response to a pilot input, the reaction lag of a mechanical system being absent.

5. Variants

The first production versions of the F-16 to enter service were the F-16A single-seat fighter and its F-16B two-seat trainer counterpart. The differences between the versions were minimal and confined to the F-16B's second cockpit and ejection seat, associated canopy and reduced internal fuel. In all other respects the versions retained the same weapons capability and the same performance envelope.

Compared with earlier aircraft programmes, the manufacturer and the USAF used a slightly different method of describing the modification state of each minor update introduced onto the production line. The block system of identification was still retained – producing designations such as F-16A-10-C for example, the final letter indicating a modification. To complicate the situation further, however, other programmes were put in place to upgrade the aircraft within the European NATO framework thus ensuring that all were cross compatible.

The first 43 production F-16s were a direct follow on from the preceding eight FSD aircraft and were powered by the F100-PW-200 turbofan engine with a rating of 55.23 kN (12,420 lb st) dry thrust and a reheat output of 105.97 kN (23,830 lb st). The 21 F-16A and 22 F-16B aircraft in this batch could be distinguished by their black radome and smaller tailplanes. Not long after the aircraft entered service its radome colour was changed to a medium grey, since pilots had complained that the earlier colour made the aircraft stand out like a sore thumb in an air-combat situation. The follow on block of

Luke AFB, the home for worldwide F-16 training operations and support. F-16D 83-175 is part of the training fleet. Note the aircraft's unusually dark radome. *(Scott Van Aken)*

Although it could be mistaken for a USAF machine, this is in fact an F-16D of the Republic of Singapore Air Force being used for training purposes at Luke AFB. The aircraft has the enlarged spine only seen on Singaporean and IDF/AF aircraft. (Scott Van Aken)

99 single-seaters and 27 two-seaters, designated as Block 5 aircraft, began to enter service during 1979. Some 169 further aircraft, including 145 single-seaters, were designated as Block 10 machines. The surviving aircraft from the earlier blocks in both European and USAF service were all brought up to Block 10 standard, but deemed to be beyond further upgrading. All were subject to the Pacer Loft avionics upgrade programmes carried out during 1982/83.

First major change

The Block 15 airframes, delivered between November 1981 and March 1985, introduced the first major change to the F-16. This was the fitment of the increased-size tailplanes, which were required to improve stability, especially during periods of extreme manoeuvring. Further stability gains were in the area of AoA attitudes and reduced lift-off rotation speeds. Other minor changes included the installation of a pair of radar warning aerials under the nose, while the AN/APG-66 radar system received an upgrade to enable it to track while it scanned. Upgrading was also carried out to the UHF radios, which received the Have Quick 1 security modification.

Under the skin, structural strengthening was applied to the wing hardpoints, allowing a further 454 kg (1,000 lb) of ordnance to be carried overall. The USAF received many of the 475 Block 15 airframes built. Diversions included 40 each to Egypt and Pakistan, 24 for Venezuela and 60 for the Netherlands.

In service, the Block 15 aircraft underwent Operational Capability Upgrades (OCUs), which saw the installation of the more reliable F100-PW-220 engine, the larger HUD from the F-16C/D and further structural reinforcement. New aircraft were also built to this standard for Belgium, Indonesia, the Netherlands, Norway, Pakistan, Singapore and Thailand.

With the appearance of improved F-16 models, some of the earlier Block 15 aircraft were found a new role. In October 1986 a conversion programme was instituted at Ogden Air Logistics Center that would involve 275 airframes being converted to F-16A/B ADF (Air Defence Fighter) standard. These airframes were for operation by the ANG in the defence of the US against intruding aircraft and cruise missiles. After the initial batch of trials aircraft had been completed, a contract for 270 further conversion kits was placed to bring the total to 279, of which 272 would be completed owing to attrition. Most of the changes involved the avionics systems, with the AN/APG-66 radar being made compatible with the AIM-7 Sparrow and the AIM-120 AMRAAM radar-guided missiles. Other modifications saw the installation of an HF radio and a 150,000-candle-power spotlight on the port side of the forward fuselage to aid in the identification of night intruders. The first upgraded F-16 ADF was rolled out in 1988 to begin flight testing, with deliveries to operational units beginning early the following year. Besides the nose-mounted spotlight, the F-16 ADF also sported other visible alterations, the primary of which was a pair of bulges at the base of the fin, housing the rudder actuators displaced by the Bendix/King AN/ARC-200 HF radio. At the other end of the airframe a pair of blade aerials was installed in front of the canopy for the Teledyne Systems Mk XII Advanced IFF system. These latter two systems were not fitted to the F-16B ADF airframes.

The ANG also took 24 F-16A/B Block 10 aircraft for service with the New York ANG based at Syracuse. Unlike the ADF version, this small batch is dedicated to the close air support role, for which wiring and mountings were

A Spangdahlem-based, AGM-88 HARM-armed F-16CJ comes in to land. *(Nick Challoner)*

installed in the centreline pylon as part of the Pave Claw modification. The other part of this modification is a gunpod housing a GAU-13A four-barrelled cannon for use against a variety of ground targets.

Production of the F-16A/B for the USAF totalled 795 airframes, consisting of 674 F-16As and 121 F-16Bs. Of these, two were built by Fokker, three were produced by SABCA and the remainder were products of Fort Worth. Production in Europe centred upon Fokker and SABCA. SABCA manufactured 96 F-16As for the BAF, the last machine being delivered in April 1985. In the Netherlands, Fokker constructed a total of 167 airframes, with the final 20 being wired for the Oude Delft Orpheus

F-16C 90-708, on the inventory of the 57th FWW, is pictured on approach to its home base at Nellis AFB. The introduction of the C/D versions presented the USAF with an improved fighter that was eventually concentrated in two roles, SEAD and attack, while retaining full air defence capability. *(Bob Archer/BBA Archive)*

One of the main goals of the USAF and multinational European F-16 programme was that of commonality between all variants of the F-16. To this end the Multi Stage Improvement Programmes and the Mid-Life Update projects were put into practice. One of the most obvious external signs of the European MLU is the aerials in front of the canopy seen on this RDAF machine. *(Jens Jensen)*

sensor pod. These aircraft are designated F-16A(R). A pair of F-16B(R) aircraft was built for training purposes. Fokker was also the main manufacturer for Norway, producing some 72 airframes for the country.

F-16C/D

Following on from the F-16A/B came the main production versions of the Fighting Falcon, these being the F-16C single-seat and F-16D two-seat versions, both being introduced into service in 1984. The new variant was capable of full all-weather operation and was compatible with the BVR AIM-7 Sparrow and AIM-120 AMRAAM from the outset. The introduction of all-weather and BVR-missile capability came after experience gained in operations over Europe, where the earlier versions had struggled in bad weather. The limited capability of the F-16 in typical European weather had been pointed out when the F-16 FSD made its European test and evaluation flights, but it had taken a while for this to sink in.

The new standard was seen originally as no more than an upgrade, designated Block 25 as part of MSIP Stage II. However, such were the changes embodied that the new block was redesignated in 1981. Production of the F-16C/D has been concentrated upon the needs of the USAF and the export market, none being diverted to the four European participants. The export versions went to Bahrain, Egypt, Greece, Israel, South Korea and Turkey, the latter two orders involving some local production.

Externally, the F-16C/D is very similar to the F-16A/B, except for an increase in the size of the lower fin assembly, which also mounts a small aerial. As well as enhancing the stability of the Fighting Falcon, the larger lower fin provided space for the installation of the US Navy-sponsored Airborne Self Protection Jammer (ASPJ). However, this equipment never proceeded beyond the development stage, since the USAF part of the programme ran into controversy during 1989–90. For the USAF, ASPJ was subsequently abandoned, eventually being replaced by the AN/ALQ-178.

The changes between the F-16A/B and F-16C/D are mostly internal. Starting from the nose, the AN/APG-66 radar was replaced by the AN/APG-68(V) multi-mode radar by retrofit to early Blocks. This features better range, sharper target resolution and expanded operating parameters. To support these improvements, signals are generated by a planar array that can be modulated for air-to-air modes, including range while scan; uplook and velocity search; single target tracking; raid cluster resolution; and track while scan for up to ten targets. The added BVR capability includes a high-PRF mode for the semi-active guidance of any BVR missile. For air-to-ground operations, the selectable modes include maritime tracking; fixed and moving target tracking; ground mapping; Doppler beam

sharpening; ranging; beacon and target freezing. The beacon mode has a dual function, having a pure navigation role and applying offsets during bombing runs. Available maritime modes include real beam mapping; sea search; fixed target tracking; and ground moving target indication and tracking.

To control all these extra modes and to present the incoming data, the pilot of an F-16C has a HUD of increased area which is operated by a keypad console at its base. On the F-16A/B this console was located to the left of the pilot. To further assist the pilot in data handling there is a display alongside the HUD.

The first Block 25 F-16C made its maiden flight on 19 June 1984 when 83-1118 took to the skies. The aircraft was delivered to the USAF one month later. Full-scale production of the F-16C/D Fighting Falcon began in December 1984, deliveries to service operators beginning soon afterwards. The path of introduction was not smooth, however, since problems during certain aspects of the flight regime began to occur. Airframe problems were quickly discounted, the fault being traced to bugs in the flight control software. There was a slight delay in countering this problem, since recoding software for aircraft is a far harder task than implementing the airframe tweaks that were traditionally the norm.

New engine for Block 30

The Pratt & Whitney F100-PW-200 powered the F-16C/D initially, but its dominance was soon challenged when the USAF decided to adopt the Alternative Fighter Engine programme. This brought General Electric on board as a second engine supplier, the theory being that each fiscal year would see engine contracts being awarded to whichever manufacturer offered the best package. General Electric's powerplant is based on the F101 DFE and is designated F110. The first appearance of the alternative engine occurred in February 1984, when General Electric was awarded a contract that covered 75 per cent of the Fiscal Year 1985 F-16C/D build. Pratt & Whitney powered the remaining 25 per cent with its upgraded and improved F100-PW-220 engine. In order that some sense could be made of engine spares logistics it was ordered that no unit should, unless absolutely necessary, operate F-16s fitted with different powerplants.

Concerted efforts resolved any logistics problems allowing full-scale deliveries to ensue. Overseas units such as the 'Wolfpack' in South Korea were among the first to receive the upgraded fighter and it took until April 1986 for a continental United States unit to equip. This was the 56th TFW based at MacDill AFB.

The first F-16s to have the General Electric engine fitted were the Block 30 series, which was also known as MSIP Stage III. Originally the production airframes retained the smaller intakes designed for the Pratt & Whitney powerplant, but the newer engine produced 128.89 kN (28,984 lb st) which is 2.22 kN (500 lb st) more than the F100 engine and so a greater mass of air was required. It took some time for the larger intake to be designed, tested and introduced into production airframes, therefore the early F-16C/D Block 30s retained the original unit. Although the larger intake improved the performance of the General Electric powerplant, the Pratt & Whitney engine cannot handle the increased mass airflow.

Smartly finished in red and white, with a grey radome and canopy frame, this AFFTC F-16B taxies out at Edwards AFB to undertake another training sortie. *(Scott Van Aken)*

In addition to the capabilities already provided in the Block 30 Fighting Falcon a further upgrade was intended for 146 aircraft. Designated Pave Claw this programme entailed the fitment of a General Electric GPU-5/A gun pod that contained a four-barrelled GAU-13A 30-mm cannon and ammunition and an improved HUD mode for ground attack. This programme would have replaced the dedicated A-16 ground attack version of the Fighting Falcon which was terminated because of technical problems.

Block 32

Following on from the Block 30 came the Block 32, which reverted to the original Pratt & Whitney powerplant. Even this had undergone a revision, however, the model being fitted being the dash 220, rated at 105.71 kN (23,770 lb st), a slightly lower output than the dash 200, but more stable and less susceptible to compressor stagnation stalling.

Block 30/32 Fighting Falcons were capable of carrying and launching the AGM-45 Shrike and AGM-88A anti-radiation missiles. Expanded air-to-air capabilities included options to carry the AIM-120 AMRAAM. Also cleared for F-16C/D usage is the Hughes AGM-65D Maverick air-to-surface missile. To support weapons delivery, navigation and flight control, the computer system had increased memory, a programmable display generator and a data entry unit. Manufacture of late

model Block 30/32 Fighting Falcons began in January 1986 with service deliveries beginning during July 1987.

Block 40/42

With production of the Block 30/32 aircraft well underway, attention turned to developing and constructing the next major advance in the F-16C/D standard. This was the Block 40/42, also known as the Night Falcon, which has enhanced night- and all-weather capabilities as part of the MSIP Stage III programme. Enhancements included the addition of LANTIRN pods, a GPS navigation receiver, provision for an upgraded AGM-88, updated APG-68(V) radar, digital flight controls, automatic terrain following and a diffractive optics HUD. Block 40 aircraft featured the GE powerplant, Block 42s having P&W engines. Complementing these improvements was a further increase in the aircraft's structural strength, raising overall basic weight from 12202 kg to 12928 kg (26,900 lb to 28,500 lb) and improving the aircraft's 9-g rating with increased

loads. Changes were also made to the main undercarriage legs, whose overall length was increased to improve ground clearance when the LANTIRN pods are fitted. When the pods were first installed they blocked the landing lights on the main gear legs, these lights therefore being moved to the nose leg. A final undercarriage enhancement was an increased wheel size, which reduced the airframe's 'foot print'. Bulged main gear doors were fitted to cover the wider wheels.

LANTIRN is possibly the greatest advance applied to the F-16. It consists of two separate pods mounted under the intakes, the left one containing the AAQ-13 navigation system complete with TFR, and that to the right containing the AAQ-14 targeting system. To ensure that the F-16 gains maximum benefit from both pods, they are fully integrated with the aircraft's flight controls. Thus, the TFR in the navigation pod flies the aircraft in 'hands off'

This image reveals the eagle pattern painted on the undersurfaces of 'Thunderbird 6' as it makes its approach to land. *(Damien Burke)*

mode when selected. The AAQ-13 pod was the first to appear, since the targeting pod was delayed by technical problems.

Block 50/52

The next version to appear is the current production variant known as Block 50/52. Block 50 aircraft are powered by the General Electric engine, in this case the -129, while Block 52 machines are fitted with the -229 P&W engine, which is lighter and more powerful than earlier versions and began test flying at Edwards AFB in 1990 in aircraft 81-0816. Block 50/52 aircraft have improved capabilities, including full integration with the AGM-88 HARM, which uses the Raytheon AN/ASQ-213

F-16A FA-116, of No.10 Wing, FAB, in landing configuration with its airbrakes open and leading and trailing flaps deployed. *(Damien Burke)*

Wearing 'Marines' titles and an unusual striped scheme, this F-16N illustrates that the US Marine Corps also provided funding for the DACT programme, although its input was not enough to save the operational units. *(Scott Van Aken)*

HARM Targeting System that entered USAF service in 1994. To support these new weapons the radar has been upgraded to AN/APG-68(V5) standard, with advanced signal processing capabilities. A further integrated addition is the AN/ALR-65M radar warning receiver for passive detection, while active defence is provided by AN/ALE-47 chaff and flare dispensers. The first of this production sequence was delivered for USAF service in November 1991.

In December 1992 Lockheed Aerospace bought out the General Dynamics Fort Worth production division for $1.525 billion dollars, later becoming Lockheed Martin in June 1995 after merging with Martin Marietta. After purchase the plant became known as the Lockheed Fort Worth Company, where manufacture of the F-16 continued.

Block 60

Representing Lockheed Martin's current thinking concerning the development path of the F-16 is the Block 60 version. This builds on the previous upgrades included in the Block 50/52 machines by adding an agile-beam radar,

internal FLIR targeting system, advanced internal ECM systems, improved glass cockpit and an enhanced performance engine that can be a derivative of the F100 or F110. Range increases are possible by the fitment of conformal fuel tanks which contain 1893 litres (416 Imp gal) of fuel. The Block 60 launch customer was the United Arab Emirates.

Special versions

The basic F-16 airframe has been subject to numerous modifications, some more exotic than others. The first modified variant was the truly remarkable F-16XL, which was first proposed by General Dynamics in February 1980 and features a radically redesigned wing. Under the designation SCAMP (Supersonic Cruise And Manoeuvring Prototype) the project took a lengthened F-16 fuselage and married it to a cranked-arrow planform wing. This wing, which allowed the tailplanes to be deleted, doubled the wing area of the aircraft and would hopefully ensure supersonic cruise performance.

As this was initially a private venture, General Dynamics put up the funding for the modification of a pair of redundant F-16 FSD airframes. It was joined by the USAF in late 1980 to create a joint test programme. This cleared the third and sixth FSD airframes for conversion purposes. To accommodate the new wing the fuselage was lengthened to just over 16.46 m (54 ft), the wing being blended into this new assembly. The cranked-arrow wing features a large amount of carbonfibre composite materials. These reduced weight and also gave pointers to the aircraft industry on how to employ these materials to their best advantage. Another benefit gained from the area increase was the capability to mount up to seventeen stores pylons.

The first conversion, 75-0749, now redesignated as an F-16XL, made its first flight on 3 July 1982 piloted by James McKinney. This aircraft was a single-seater and was powered by an F100-PW-201 turbofan. The second airframe was converted from F-16A FSD 75-0747, although it had been converted to two-seat configuration when the forward fuselage of a redundant F-16B FSD airframe, damaged in a heavy landing, was grafted on. In contrast with the first airframe, this aircraft was powered by a General Electric F110-GE-100 engine and made its maiden flight on 29 October 1982, crewed by Alex Wolf and James McKinney. Initial handling reports concerning the F-16XLs revealed an aircraft that performed in a completely different manner to the standard production F-16, being very smooth during high speed runs at low level.

General Dynamics made only one concerted effort to sell the F-16XL to the USAF when it was entered in the Advanced Tactical Fighter competition to replace the ageing F-111. Its rival was a modified McDonnell Douglas F-15B two-seater that eventually emerged as the winner in February 1984. In its production form this development of the trainer version of the Eagle is known as the F-15E Strike Eagle. Had the F-16XL won the competition it would have been offered in two forms. The single-seater would have been known as the F-16E, while its two-seat counterpart would have been designated F-16F. Having lost the competition the two airframes were returned to Fort Worth in mid 1985 for storage, having completed 437 and 361 flights, respectively. Unfortunately for General Dynamics, the F-16XL did not quite achieve its goal, which was supersonic cruise without the use of afterburner.

This, however, was not the end for the two aircraft. In late 1988 they were removed from storage, refurbished and handed over to NASA for investigation into airflow behaviour over aerofoils of different shapes. The first flight of a NASA-sponsored F-16XL was undertaken on 9 March 1989, after which it was delivered to the NASA Dryden Flight Research Center at Edwards AFB. Once flight performance criteria had been established, the first aircraft had a titanium section grafted on to its left wing. This new section features thousands of minuscule

laser-cut holes that bleed off the turbulent boundary layer air. This process is known as active suction. It syphons off the air to provide a more stable airflow and is part of research into laminar flow. The first flight of the modified F-16XL was undertaken on 3 May 1990 in the hands of test pilot Steve Ishmael. The second aircraft was passed onto the NASA research centre at Langley, where it remains.

Specifications for the F-16XL include a wing span of 10.44 m (34 ft 3 in); a wing area of 60.01 m² (646 sq ft); a fuselage length of 16.51 m (54 ft 2 in) and a height of 5.36 m (17 ft 7 in). Basic fuelled weight is 19505 kg (43,000 lb) with a maximum clean weight of 21773 kg (48,000 lb). The

This pair of Esk 727 F-16As was photographed at the RDAF's Aalborg base. The nearest machine, toting a pair of wing tip AIM-9 Sidewinders and a centreline fuel tank, is E-197. (Jens Jensen)

maximum speed for the F100-powered version is Mach 2.05 at 12192 m (40,000 ft). Armament, when fitted, included one internal 20-mm M61A1 cannon, with one AIM-9 Sidewinder missile on each wing tip. An external load of 6804 kg (15,000 lb) could be carried on the 17 pylons.

Celebrating 50 years of No. 31 Sqn, FAB, this F-16A is complete with unusual Tiger Meet artwork on its fin. (Nick Challoner)

Above: Slowing and turning with its airbrakes partially deployed, this NATO-bedecked F-16A has dummy AIM-120s at its wing tips, while underwing an ACMI pod and Sidewinder are sported. The other wing pylons are occupied by fuel tanks. *(Damien Burke)*

Below: F-16A MLU J-016 of the KLu sports the 2002 air show display colour scheme. In contrast with previous such finishes, the wing tip smoke generator pods are painted to blend in. On previous occasions the pods retained their gaudy dayglo finish. *(Bob Archer/BBA Archive)*

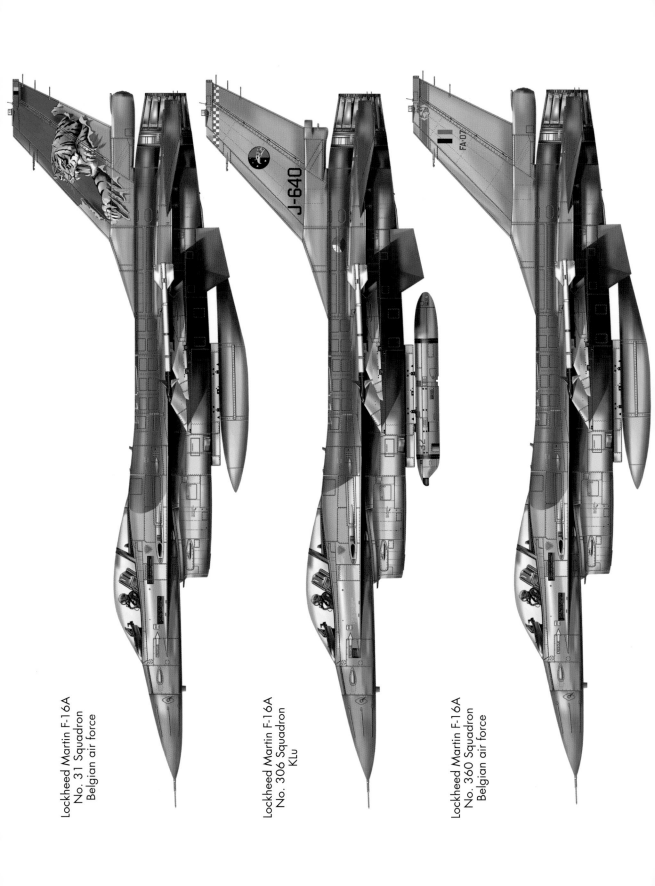

Lockheed Martin F-16A
No. 31 Squadron
Belgian air force

Lockheed Martin F-16A
No. 306 Squadron
Klu

Lockheed Martin F-16A
No. 360 Squadron
Belgian air force

J-640

FA-07

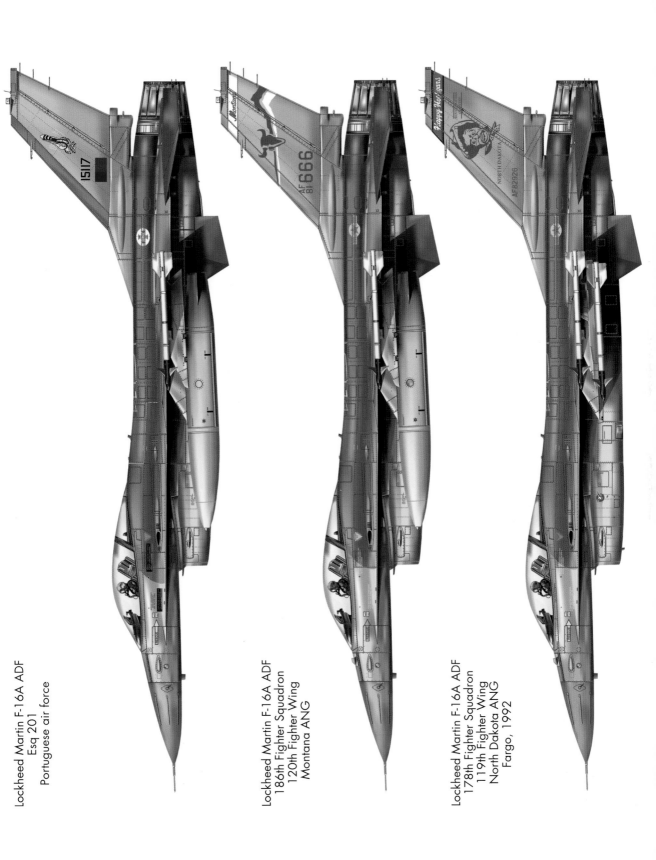

Lockheed Martin F-16A ADF
Esq 201
Portuguese air force

Lockheed Martin F-16A ADF
186th Fighter Squadron
120th Fighter Wing
Montana ANG

Lockheed Martin F-16A ADF
178th Fighter Squadron
119th Fighter Wing
North Dakota ANG
Fargo, 1992

The tail code 'WW' signifies that this air defence-optimised F-16C is on the inventory of the 432nd FW, not as might be imagined the more famous Wild Weasel wing that once operated out of George AFB, Georgia. *(USAF)*

F-16/79

Although the F-16 has two different engines available as standard, it has been the recipient of others for evaluation purposes. The first of these evaluation variants was designated F-16/79 and was conceived in February 1977 at the behest of President Jimmy Carter. It was felt that some countries should not receive the latest technology in arms exports and included among this non-exportable technology was the F100. Exempt from this policy were the four NATO partner countries;

Above: F-16XL NASA 848 was originally 75-0747, a single-seat F-16 FSD vehicle. In this view the aircraft is fitted with a variety of wing sections for various aerodynamic trials which included laminar flow control experiments. *(via NASA)*

Right: In later years the first YF-16 was used by the Flight Dynamics Laboratory for Control Configured Vehicle trials, although in this shot the fins normally located under the intake are missing. *(Scott Van Aken)*

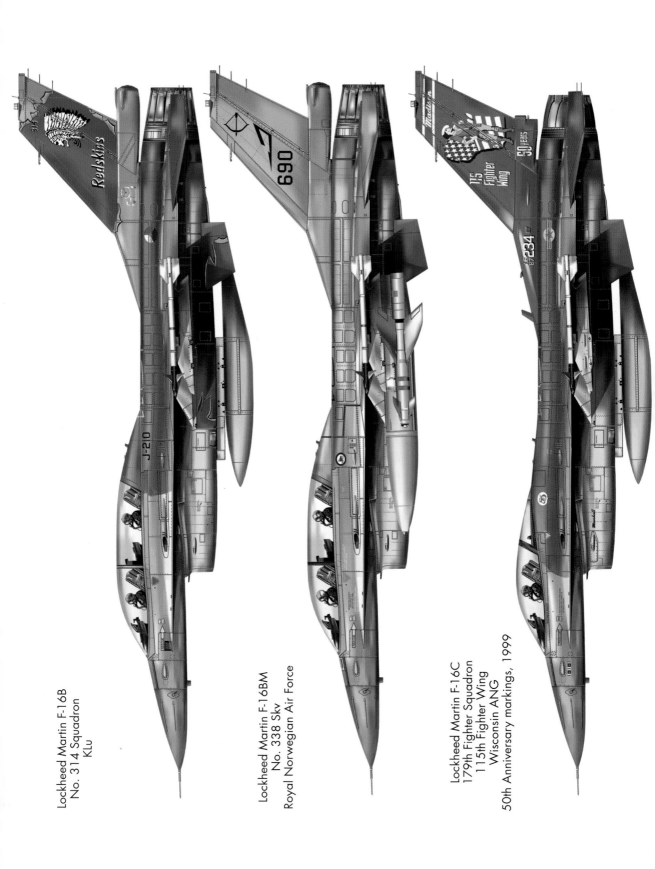

Lockheed Martin F-16B
No. 314 Squadron
KLu

Lockheed Martin F-16BM
No. 338 Skv
Royal Norwegian Air Force

Lockheed Martin F-16C
179th Fighter Squadron
115th Fighter Wing
Wisconsin ANG
50th Anniversary markings, 1999

Lockheed Martin F-16C Block 30
140th Fighter Wing
Colorado ANG

Lockheed Martin F-16C Block 30
149th Fighter Squadron
192nd Fighter Wing
In the colours of a P-51D-15-NA of the
328th FS, 352nd FG, 1944, flown by
top-scoring Mustang ace Maj. George
Preddy with 26.83 victories

Lockheed Martin F-16C Block 30
114th Fighter Wing
South Dakota ANG

The colourful fin markings belie the warlike purpose of this F-16C of the Aviano wing. It has AIM-120 missiles on its wing tips, AIM-9 Sidewinders on the outer underwing pylons and bombs on the wing centre pylons. (USAF)

Israel as a special case and eventually South Korea, as compensation for pending US troop withdrawals. Also added to this list was the Iranian air force since the Shah was seen as a bulwark against communist incursions into the Middle East. Other countries, such as Jordan, found themselves being turned down for the F-16.

Arms sales are of course a great leveller of policy, thus a down-graded version of the F-16 was put forward for export to those less-favoured countries. To produce this aircraft General Dynamics teamed up with General Electric to investigate installing the ubiquitous J79 engine. The revamped design was first revealed in November 1979, with its engine being designated J79-GE-119. The airframe chosen to trial this installation was F-16B, 75-0752, which required a reshaped intake to accommodate the J79's reduced mass air flow requirement. Another modification required to accommodate the J79,

which was 45.2 cm (18 in) longer than the F100, was an extension of the rear fuselage. This also needed a steel heat shield to contain the extra heat generated by the new powerplant. To make this new version attractive to its intended market, it was recommended that the production version be sold at a price $1 million below that of the F-16A.

The first flight of the F-16/79 was undertaken on 29 October 1980 piloted by company test pilot James McKinney. Although the J79-powered F-16 completed its flight trials successfully, the air forces invited to review it rejected the aircraft completely. The given reason was a reduction in performance caused by the reduced engine thrust and the weight of the extra steel engine shielding in comparison with the standard fighter. The whole project was subsequently dropped when President Carter revoked his original policy decision and allowed a limited export of standard F-16s, a policy which was further expanded by President Reagan when he assumed office.

Another airframe that was involved in engine trials was the first F-16A FSD, 75-0745, which became the test-bed for the F101 DFE engine derived from that developed for the Rockwell

B-1 bomber. The first flight of the modified fighter was undertaken on 19 December 1980. Problems with intake vibrations required some fixes before the flight test programme could continue. Eventually the aircraft flew 58 sorties which involved 75 flying hours. Although the tests were successful the trials were ended in July 1981 with no orders forthcoming. Eventually, however, the engine was developed into the F110 engine which would power the F-16 in the future.

The 57th FWW operates the F-16 in the DACT role, therefore, its aircraft sport a range of schemes such as this Soviet-style effort. (USAF)

MATV/VISTA

One of the most unusual projects carried out using the F-16 is the MATV (Multi-Axis Thrust Vectoring) and VISTA (Variable-Stability In-Flight Simulator Test Aircraft) programmes. The aircraft used for these trials was a loaned USAF F-16D Block 30 which began work in its

Lockheed Martin F-16C Block 32
302nd Fighter Squadron
944th Fighter Wing
50th Anniversary markings, 1998
In the wartime colours of a P-51C of the 332nd
FG, 15th Air Force, Tuskegee Airmen

Lockheed Martin F-16C Block 40
68th Fighter Squadron
347th Fighter Wing

Lockheed Martin F-16C Block 40
16th Air Force

Lockheed Martin F-16C Block 40
No. 105 Squadron
IDF/AF

Lockheed Martin F-16C Block 50
79th Fighter Squadron

Lockheed Martin F-16D
46th Test Wing

Lockheed Martin F-16D Block 42
308th Fighter Squadron
56th Fighter Wing
Luke AFB

Lockheed Martin F-16D Block 50
151 Filo
Turkish air force

Lockheed Martin F-16D Block 52
No. 143 Squadron
Republic of Singapore Air Force

fully modified form in July 1993. Not only has this aircraft featured modified flight controls in its VISTA form, the nozzle for the F110 engine is also variable in direction when employed on MATV trials. Although not intended for operational combat duties the VISTA fighter has demonstrated that extreme angles of attack are possible with such an aircraft, although the MATV programme was stopped after just five test flights.

F-16/CCV

Several F-16s have been modified for development work. The first of these was the F-16/CCV (Control Configured Vehicle) which involved the conversion of the first YF-16, 72-1567, during December 1975. The F-16/CCV

is unlike any other aircraft in that it can change direction in one plane without moving into another; thus the aircraft can turn without banking. This is possible because the flight controls were decoupled and supplemented by two fins located below the intake, while the flaperons were modified to operate in conjunction with the tailerons.

The maiden flight of the F-16/CCV was completed on 16 March 1976, with pilot David Thigpen at the controls. The flight test schedule was interrupted on 24 June 1976 when the aircraft was crash-landed on the grass after the engine failed on approach. Repaired, the F-16/CCV continued test flying until finally being grounded on 31 June 1977 after 87 sorties covering some 125 flying hours.

This four-ship formation is from the 432nd FW based at Misawa AB, Japan. The aircraft are configured for the air defence role with AIM-120 AMRAAM missiles for long-range interception on their wing tip rails, and AIM-9 Sidewinders for closer work underwing. (USAF)

F-16/AFTI

The F-16/AFTI (Advanced Fighter Technology Integration) was a direct follow on from the F-16/CCV. Jointly sponsored by the Flight Dynamics Laboratory and Air Force Systems Command, the airframe chosen for conversion by General Dynamics was F-16A FSD, 75-0750. Work began in 1979 and culminated with the first flight of the AFTI on 10 July 1982. Externally ATFI was similar to the CCV, but featured much enhanced electronics in a bulged spine.

Intensive flight trials lasted from 1983 to 1987, before the aircraft became involved in the A-16 ground-attack programme. Over the years various upgrades have been undertaken to the airframe, including the replacement of the original wing by one of Block 25 standard. The airframe was also modified to carry various navigation and targeting pods, including the Pave Penny laser-designator.

Wearing the tail code of Shaw AFB on its fin, this F-16C is dedicated to the SEAD role as the AGM-88 HARM missiles on the wing centre pylons testify. *(USAF)*

RF-16

Reconnaissance is a very important part of any air force's repertoire. The primary vehicle in USAF service was the ageing RF-4C Phantom, the replacement of which was seen as a priority. The first moves to replace the Phantom were undertaken in 1988 by the USAF. General Dynamics proposed the RF-16, fitted with the ATARS (Advanced Tactical Air Reconnaissance System), a multi-sensor pod that would be carried on the centreline pylon. This system was capable of delivering real-time information to battlefield commanders via a digital downlink. Although the system proved successful, the RF-16 was not adopted for USAF service.

This underside view of a landing KLu F-16 reveals an ACMI pod under the port wing, while a ballast pod of similar size and shape is mounted on the opposite side. *(Bob Archer/BBA Archive)*

Agile Falcon

When the Su-27 and MiG-29 appeared in the Soviet inventory, General Dynamics proposed an upgraded version of the F-16 to combat them. Beginning in 1984, the Agile Falcon programme added to the basic fighter a wing of increased area and uprated engines from both General Electric and Pratt & Whitney – both modifications were being promoted as part of MSIP IV. With the F-15 Eagle in service in great numbers, however, the Agile Falcon project found no takers.

General Dynamics made one more attempt to sell Agile Falcon, this time as a low cost alternative to the Lockheed Martin F-22

This 'Boss Bird' F-16C from the 52nd FW, Spangdahlem AB in Germany, shows many of the elements that make the F-16 design a winner, not least of which is the type's diminutive airframe, into which much equipment and fuel is crammed. *(Bob Archer/BBA Archive)*

This Spangdahlem-based F-16C is replete with weapons and defensive systems. The centreline pylon has an ECM pod installed, the wing tips sport AIM-120 missiles and just inboard are AIM-9s for short-range work. On the wing centre stations are AGM-88 HARM rounds, while the inner pylons are toting fuel tanks. Completing the external inventory is the HTS pod under the intake. *(USAF)*

Advanced Tactical Fighter for both the USAF and NATO partners. Although the USAF did express some interest during 1987, the whole project was put on hold when the Berlin Wall came down, an event which was followed by a reduction in front-line strength.

The USAF and General Dynamics made further efforts to extend the usefulness of the F-16 by improving its ground-attack capabilities. As the A-16, it was intended that Block 30/32 airframes would be reworked for an enhanced ground-attack role to replace the A-10 Thunderbolt II, which was seen as incapable of surviving in a hi-tech battlefield environment. It was at this point that inter-service rivalries between the US Army, USMC and USAF came into play, the result being that two wings of A-10s were retained for attack purposes. This resulted in the A-16 being cancelled although the USAF subsequently investigated equipping 400 F-16C Block 30

airframes with a centreline gunpod and updated software which would allow them to perform the close air support mission.

F-16ES

The IDF/AF was the progenitor of the next version of the Fighting Falcon. Known as the F-16ES (Extended Strategic), this machine featured conformal fuel tanks (CFTs) on its upper fuselage. These extended the type's range to 1650 km (1,025 miles) with a weapon load of 1814 kg (4,000 lb). Unfortunately, the ES was beaten to the IDF/AF contract by the F-15I Eagle. However, the project was not completely dead, since the USAF and Lockheed resurrected it in late 1994 and extensively tested F-16C 83-1120 with dummy tanks.

Cheaper and advanced versions

Three other versions of the F-16 have been proposed to the USAF since Lockheed took over.

A consortium led by Mitsubishi has developed the F-2 in close partnership with Lockheed Martin. F-2 is not a straight F-16 copy, since the airframe has been considerably redesigned and much of the avionics content is indigenous. *(LMTAS)*

The first was intended to keep the Fort Worth production line open after the USAF was scheduled to receive its last F-16 in 1997 and foreign orders would have been completed in 1999, although the F-16 has continued to attract orders from both home and abroad. The proposal was to produce a quantity of F-16 Block 50 aircraft with a reduced price tag, keeping the line open and filling a perceived shortfall in the inventory of 100 aircraft.

Another F-16 version, known as the F-16X, was proposed as a cheaper multi-role fighter that was postulated for possible service in 2010. The airframe would inherit the wing of the F-22, the vertical fin being completely omitted. To prepare the way for the F-16X some of the proposed

mission equipment has begun to appear in the Block 50 aircraft. This includes an upgraded glass cockpit, and improved navigation, radar and warning systems. A further improvement is proposed for Block 60 aircraft, where a bulged spine would be incorporated containing an increased fuel load.

The final outing for the F-16 for USAF purposes was the F-16AT, or Falcon 21, which was proposed as a cheaper alternative to the Lockheed Martin F-22. It would be based on the F-16XL, with the original cranked-arrow wing replaced by one trapezoidal in shape.

Mitsubishi F-2

The Mitsubishi F-2 for the Japan Air Self Defence Force is a derivative of the F-16 produced in conjunction with Lockheed Martin. The programme began in October 1987, with a prototype flying for the first time in January 1995. Since that date the type has been cleared for mass production and has begun to enter service.

Appendix 1. Weapons and Stores

When the F-16 was first conceived its initial role was seen purely as a lightweight fighter. To reflect this fact, the armament consisted of just a fuselage-mounted cannon and a pair of wing tip-mounted AIM-9 Sidewinders, in association with a basic gun-ranging radar. As the design progressed a single underwing pylon per side was added, quickly followed by a centreline station. Once the F-16 design had proven itself further improvements were put in hand. The primary of these was the installation of the APG-66 multi-mode radar. In addition to the radar, a strengthened wing structure was added which allowed the amount of pylons to be increased to three per wing. This brought the total weapons pylons up to nine.

Constant across all front-line versions of the F-16 is the General Dynamics 20-mm M61A1 Vulcan six-barrel Gatling gun, which is supplied with 511 rounds of M50 ammunition. Maximum rate of fire is 6,000 rounds per minute, the rate being selectable by a switch in the cockpit. Drive for the cannon's rotary barrels is taken from the aircraft's hydraulic system, while firing control is undertaken electronically. Although the Vulcan cannon is a proven and reliable weapon, its installation in the F-16 initially ran into problems. These came to light in September 1979, when firing was temporarily forbidden. Two incidents had occurred in which gun firing resulted in uncommanded aircraft yawing movements. The cause of this problem was an accelerometer in the flight control system, which

was being affected by the vibrations caused when the gun fired. The accelerometer fed false data into the flight control computer, which initiated the yaw movements. Simply insulating the accelerometer from vibration solved the problem. All operational F-16s delivered to that date were modified during 1980.

Air-to-air missiles

Reflecting its early air defence roots, the Fighting Falcon has always been kept up to date with the latest air-to-air missiles. The first type carried was the AIM-9 Sidewinder. The weapon is guided using an IR-seeking head which, in the later versions, is capable of all-aspect targeting. This was a vast improvement on the earlier models, which were only capable of locking on to an aircraft's primary heat source, its engine. Following on from the Sidewinder came the Raytheon AIM-7 Sparrow semi-active radar-homing (SARH) missile, which was intended for BVR interception. Succeeding the Sparrow in front-line service came the far more capable AIM-120 AMRAAM which can replace the Sidewinder if required. AAMs are carried on the wing tip rails and the pylons immediately inboard. In the air defence role, as practised by the ANG, the Sparrow is still in normal usage although the AIM-120 is mooted as a replacement.

Ground-attack mission

When the Fighting Falcon added the ability to attack ground targets to its repertoire, courtesy of the air-to-ground modes incorporated into its APG-66 radar, a full spread of 'iron' bombs and missiles was added to the type's inventory. The missiles cover two distinct roles. The first is general ground attack, while the other is anti-radar. For the former task both primary versions of the AGM-65 Maverick can be utilised, one is optically guided, AGM-65A/B, while the other relies on IR, AGM-65D, for target lock-on. In the single-seat F-16 the latter is the preferred weapon, since the optical-guidance version increases the cockpit workload considerably.

In SEAD (Suppression of Enemy Air Defences) missions, the primary targets fired at are radar detection and guidance systems. When the F-16 first undertook this role it was armed with the AGM-45 Shrike. This ageing weapon was eventually replaced by the AGM-88 HARM (High Speed Anti-Radiation Missile), which is now the preferred anti-radar missile for both the USAF and US Navy. The normal pylon for the carriage of these weapons is the centre one under each wing.

Three basic low drag 'iron' bomb versions are cleared for F-16 use, these being the Mk 82, Mk 83 (IDF/AF) and Mk 84, rated at 500 lb (227 kg), 1,000 lb (454 kg) and 2,000 lb (907 kg), respectively. Further unguided bombs include the Mk 82 'Snakeye' retarded 500-lb weapon, the M117 750-lb (340-kg) high-drag bomb (IDF/AF), which is leaving USAF service, and the usual range of cluster bombs. To capitalise on the Fighting Falcon's radar guidance modes and the capabilities of the LANTIRN system the aircraft can carry laser-guided versions of the Mk 82, 83 and 84 bombs for more accurate destruction of targets. Also in this category are the GBU-15 (Guided Bomb Unit-15) and the HOBO smart bomb. Further 'smart' weapons have recently begun to be deployed by the Fighting Falcon fleet, these including the cross service JDAM (Joint Direct Attack Munition).

Other stores cleared for use by the F-16 include the SUU-25 flare pod and the SUU-20 training pod. The latter incorporates both a machine-gun package and bomblets for target practice. These pods are normally carried on the wing pylons, the centreline station normally being home to the ALQ-131 ECM pod on those aircraft that do not have internal jamming systems installed. Trials on new weapons have also been undertaken, some being adopted for regular service, while others were very much proof of concept. One of the first was the GEPOD (General Electric Pod) 30-mm gunpod which added extra firepower to the F-16. Its ammunition was limited, however, and with its rounds expended it became no more than dead weight. Given the plethora of weapons already cleared for the F-16, plus the effectiveness of its internal cannon, the pod was soon consigned to history.

Other targeting pods developed for the F-16 include the AAQ-14 Sharpshooter, a downgraded LANTIRN, which has been deployed by Bahrain and the IDF/AF. The latter also fits the indigenous Rafael Litening IR pod to its aircraft. A further batch of these pods, jointly produced by Northrop Grumman and Rafael, is being procured to equip the F-16 Block 25, 30, 32, 40 and 42s aircraft of AFRES and the ANG, with which it will be named as the Precision Attack Targeting Pod. In Europe the Netherlands mounts the Marconi Atlantic for navigation use, carried alongside ten Lockheed Martin targeting pods with improved TV capability that were delivered during 2000. Although the ATLIS II pod was not adopted by USAF, the Thomson CSF product was purchased by Pakistan.

Although the F-16 has been cleared to use the greater majority of weapons in both the USAF and NATO inventories, some countries have developed and deployed weapons for their own specific purposes. One of the first was Norway, which required that its F-16 fleet be capable of carrying and launching an indigenous anti-shipping missile. Designed and built by Kongsberg Vapenfabrikk, the Penguin 3 is a development of a ground-launched anti-shipping weapon and entered service in 1987. Trials were undertaken by the USAF, by which the missile was designated AGM-119, although no USAF contracts were forthcoming. All of the Fighting Falcons in the RNoAF inventory are capable of carrying this weapon, although normal practice is to have only one squadron dedicated to its deployment.

The KLu deploys a non-standard reconnaissance pod on its F-16 fleet. This is the Orpheus pod, which replaces the version developed for the F-104G Starfighter for use in the tactical role, and is carried on the fuselage centreline pylon. Aircraft dedicated to using this pod are designated F-16A(R).

Outside of NATO, other nations have also developed or deployed alternative weapons. One of these is Pakistan, whose air force is subject to embargoes of both complete aircraft and equipment. To counteract the deficiencies

in AIM-9 Sidewinder deliveries from the USA, the country decided to adopt the French-produced MATRA R550 Magic 2 AAM. Already a mature weapon in French service, integration and test firing of the missile from a PAF F-16 was undertaken in May 1989, with deployment taking place soon after.

Israel is another independent nation that has seen the need to develop indigenous weapons. The Raphael Python 3 is a direct replacement for the AIM-9 Sidewinder and is carried on the same wing tip rails. Entry into service was rushed so that the pre-production rounds could be used against Syrian air force fighters during the Israeli incursion into the Lebanon during 1982. Such was the success of these rounds that full-scale production was started almost immediately, with Israel claiming that the weapon is faster, more manoeuvrable and has better range than the AIM-9 Sidewinder.

Appendix 2. Production Details

Serial	Version	Notes	Serial	Version	Notes
72-1567/1568	YF-16	'1567 modified for CCV tests			'0750 modified as AFTI test-bed
75-0745/0750	FSD F-16A	'0745 modified as F-16/101, on display at Wright-Patterson AFB marked as 79-0317	75-0751/0752	FSD F-16B	'0752 modified as Wild Weasel test-bed and later as F-16/79
		'0747 modified as F-16XL/B; to NASA as 848	78-0001/0021	F-16A Block 1	
			78-0022/0027	F-16A Block 5	
			78-0038/0076	F-16A Block 5	
			78-0077/0098	F-16B Block 1	
		'0749 modified as F-16XL/A; to NASA as 849	78-0099/0115	F-16B Block 5	
			78-0116/0161	F-16A	built by SABCA for Belgium (FA-01/FA-46)

Serial	Version	Notes	Serial	Version	Notes
78-0162/0173	F-16B	built by SABCA for Belgium (FB-01/FB-12)	80-3588/3595	F-16B Block 15	built by SABCA for Belgium (FB-13/20)
78-0174/0203	F-16A Block 1	built by SABCA for Denmark (E-174/E-203)	80-3596/3611	F-16A Block 1	built by SABCA for Denmark (E-596/611)
78-0204/0211	F-16B Block 1	built by SABCA for Denmark (ET-204/ET-211)	80-3612/3615	F-16B Block 1	built by SABCA for Denmark (ET-612/615)
78-0212/0258	F-16A	built by Fokker for Holland (J-212/J-258)built	80-3616/3648	F-16A	built by Fokker for Holland (J-316/348)
78-0259/0271	F-16B	built by Fokker for Holland (J-259/J-271) '0259 became J-259 as first Fokker-built F-16	80-3649/3657	F-16B	built by Fokker for Holland (J-649/657)
			80-3658/3688	F-16A	built by Fokker for Norway (658/688)
78-0272/0300	F-16A	built by Fokker for Norway (272/300)	80-3689/3693	F-16B	built by Fokker for Norway (689/693)
78-0301/0307	F-16B	built by Fokker for Norway (301/307)	81-0643/0661	F-16A Block 15	to Egypt under *Peace Vector* (9306/9324)
78-0308/0467	F-16A	ordered by Iran but cancelled; first 55 serials were reallocated to Israel	81-0662	F-16B Block 15	to Egypt under *Peace Vector* (9206)
78-0308/0354	F-16A		81-0663/0811	F-16A Block 15	
78-0355/0362	F-16B	to Israel	81-0812/0822	F-16B Block 15	
79-0288/0331	F-16A Block 5		81-0864/0881	F-16A	built by Fokker for Holland (J-864/881)
79-0332/0409	F-16A Block 10	'0408 converted to GF-16A	81-0882	F-16B	built by Fokker for Holland (J-882)
79-0410/0419	F-16B Block 5				
79-0420/0432	F-16B Block 10		81-0883	F-16B	built by Fokker for Egypt (9207)
80-0474/0540	F-16A Block 10				
80-0541/0623	F-16A Block 15		81-0884/0885	F-16B	built by Fokker for Holland (J-884/J-885)
80-0624/0634	F-16B Block 10				
80-0635/0638	F-16B Block 15				
80-0639/0643	F-16A Block 15	to Egypt under *Peace Vector* (9301/9305)	81-0899/0930	F-16A	to Pakistan (701/728); '0927/0930 cancelled
80-0644/0648	F-16B Block 15	to Egypt under *Peace Vector* (9201/9205)	81-0931/0938	F-16B	to Pakistan (601/608)
80-0649/0668	F-16A	to Israel	81-1061	F-16A	to Egypt
80-3538/3546	F-16A	built by SABCA for Belgium (FA-47/55)	81-1504/1507	F-16B	to Pakistan
			82-0900/1025	F-16A Block 15	'0976 to NASA
80-3547/3587	F-16A Block 15	built by SABCA for Belgium (FA-56/96)	82-1026/1049	F-16B Block 15	to Egypt under *Peace Vector*
			82-1050/1052	F-16A	to Venezuela (1041, 0051, 6611)

Serial	Version	Notes	Serial	Version	Notes
82-1053/1055	F-16B	to Venezuela (1715, 2179, 9581)	87-0001	F-16B Block 15	built by SABCA for Belgium (FB-21)
82-1056/1065	F-16A Block 15	to Egypt under *Peace Vector* (9325/9334)	87-0004/0008	F-16A Block 15	built by Fokker for Denmark (E-004/008)
83-1066/1117	F-16A Block 15		87-0022	F-16B Block 15	built by Fokker for Denmark (ET-022)
83-1166/1173	F-16B Block 15				
83-1186/1188	F-16A	to Venezuela as 8900, 0678, 3260	87-0046/0056	F-16A Block 15	built by SABCA for Belgium (FA-102/112)
83-1189/1191	F-16B	to Venezuela as 2337, 7635, 9583	87-0057/0065	F-16A	contract cancelled
83-1192/1207	F-16A	built by Fokker for Holland (J-192/207)	87-0066/0068	F-16B	built by Fokker for Holland (J-066/068)
83-1208/1211	F-16B	built by Fokker for Holland (J-208/211)	87-0397/0400	F-16A	to Singapore as 880/883
84-1346/1357	F-16A	to Venezuela as 7268, 9068, 8924, 0094, 6023, 4226, 5422, 6426, 4827, 9864, 3648, 0220	87-0401/0404	F-16B	to Singapore as 884/887
			87-0508/0516	F-16A	built by Fokker for Holland (J-508/516)
			87-0702/0708	F-16A	to Thailand as 10306/10312
84-1358/1367	F-16A	built by Fokker for Holland (J-358/367)	87-0709	F-16B	to Thailand as 10304
84-1368/1369	F-16B	built by Fokker for Holland (J-368/369)	87-0710	F-16A	to Netherlands as J-710
85-0135/0146	F-16A	built by Fokker for Holland (J-135/146)	87-0711/0712	F-16B	to Norway as 711/712
			87-0713/0720	F-16A	to Indonesia as TS1605/TS1612
86-0054/0063	F-16A	built by Fokker for Holland (J-054/063)	87-0721/0724	F-16B	to Indonesia as TS1601/TS1604
86-0064/0065	F-16B	built by Fokker for Holland (J-064/065)	88-0001/0012	F-16A	built by Fokker for Holland (J-001/J-012)
86-0073/0077	F-16A Block 15	built by SABCA for Belgium (FA-97/101)	88-0016/0018	F-16A Block 15	built by Fokker for Denmark (E-016/018)
			88-0038/0047	F-16A Block 15	built by SABCA for Belgium (FA-113/122)
86-0197/0199	F-16B Block 15	built by Fokker for Denmark (ET-197/199)	88-0048/0049	F-16B Block 15	built by SABCA for Belgium (FB-22/23)
86-0378	F-16A	to Thailand as 10305	89-0001/0011	F-16A Block 15	built by SABCA for Belgium (FA-123/133)
86-0379/0381	F-16B	to Thailand as 10301/10303	89-0012	F-16B Block 15	built by SABCA for Belgium (FB-24)

Serial	Version	Notes
89-0013/0021	F-16A	built by Fokker for Holland (J-013/021) '0021 (J-021) was the last Fokker-built F-16
90-0942/0947	F-16A	to Pakistan as 729/734
90-0948/0952	F-16B	to Pakistan as 613/617
91-0062/0067	F-16A	to Thailand as 10313/10318
92-0404/0451	F-16A	to Pakistan as 92735/92782 beginning of Lockheed production '0404/0410 embargoed at AMARC
92-0452/0463	F-16B	to Pakistan as 91618/91629 '0452/0455 embargoed at AMARC
93-0465/0481	F-16A	to Portugal as 16101/16117
93-0482/0484	F-16B	to Portugal as 16118/16120
83-1118/1165	F-16C Block 25	'1124, '1125 converted to GF-16C
83-1174/1185	F-16D Block 25	
84-1212/1318	F-16C Block 25	
84-1319/1331	F-16D	'1330 modified as F-16R/RF-16
84-1332/1339	F-16C	to Egypt as 9501/9508
84-1340/1345	F-16D	to Egypt as 9401/9406
84-1370/1373	F-16D	to South Korea as 41370/41373
84-1374/1395	F-16C Block 25	
84-1396/1397	F-16D Block 25	
85-1384/1385	F-16D	to South Korea
85-1398/1505	F-16C Block 30/32	
85-1506/1508	F-16D Block 25	
85-1509	F-16D Block 30/32	
85-1510	F-16D Block 25	

F-16B 80-0629 is a Block 10 aircraft. It was photographed in service with the 125th FG based in Florida. *(C P Russell Smith Collection)*

Serial	Version	Notes
85-1511	F-16D Block 30/32	
85-1512	F-16D Block 25	
85-1513	F-16D Block 30/32	
85-1514/1516	F-16D Block 25	
85-1517	F-16D Block 30/32	
85-1518/1543	F-16C	to Egypt
85-1544/1570	F-16C Block 30/32	
85-1571/1573	F-16D Block 30/32	
85-1574/1583	F-16C	to South Korea as 51574/51583
85-1584/1585	F-16D	to South Korea as 51584/51585
86-0039/0041	F-16D	
86-0042/0053	F-16D Block 30/35	
86-0066/0072	F-16C Block 30B	to Turkey under *Peace Onyx I* as 86-0066/0072 first two built by Fort Worth, rest by TAI
86-0191/0196	F-16D	built by Fort Worth for Turkey
86-1586/1597	F-16C	to South Korea
86-1598/1612	F-16C Block 30	to Israel
87-0002/0003	F-16D Block 30E	built by TAI for Turkey, *Peace Onyx I*
87-0009/0018	F-16C Block 30B	built by TAI for Turkey, *Peace Onyx I*

Serial	Version	Notes
87-0019/0021	F-16C Block 30E	built by TAI for Turkey, *Peace Onyx I*
87-0217/0362	F-16C Block 30/32	
87-0363/0396	F-16D Block 30/32	
87-1653/1660	F-16C	to South Korea as 71653/71660
87-1661/1693	F-16C Block 30	to Israel as 340, 341, 344, 345, 348, 349, 350, 353, 355, 356, 360, 364, 367, 368, 371, 373, 374, 377, 378, 381, 384, 386, 388, 389, 391,393, 394, 392, 397, 388, 383, 385, 379
87-1694/1708	F-16D Block 30	to Israel as 020, 023, 030,030, 031, 034, 036, 039, 0441, 045, 046, 048, 050, 057, 061, 055
88-0013	F-16D Block 30E	built by TAI for Turkey, *Peace Onyx I*
88-0014/0015	F-16D Block 40A	built by TAI for Turkey, *Peace Onyx I*
88-0019/0032	F-16C Block 30E	built by TAI for Turkey, *Peace Onyx I*
88-0033/0037	F-16C Block 40A	built by TAI for Turkey, *Peace Onyx I*
88-0110/0143	F-16C Block 40	to Greece as 110/143
88-0144/0149	F-16D Block 40	to Greece as 144/149
88-0150/0175	F-16D	
88-0397/0550	F-16C	
88-1709/1711	F-16C Block 30	to Israel as 359, 313, 329
88-1712/1720	F-16D Block 30	to Israel as 065, 069, 070, 072, 074, 077/079, 083
89-0022/0033	F-16C Block 40A	built by TAI for Turkey, *Peace Onyx I*

Serial	Version	Notes
89-0034/0041	F-16C Block 40D	built by TAI for Turkey, *Peace Onyx I*
89-0042	F-16D Block 40A	built by TAI for Turkey, *Peace Onyx I*
89-0043/0045	F-16D Block 40D	built by TAI for Turkey, *Peace Onyx I*
89-0277	F-16C	to Israel as 502
89-0278/0279	F-16C	to Israel as 9701/9702
89-2000/2154	F-16C	
89-2155/2179	F-16D	
90-0001/0009	F-16C Block 40D	built by TAI for Turkey
90-0010/0021	F-16C Block 40F	built by TAI for Turkey
90-0022/0024	F-16D Block 40F	built by TAI for Turkey
90-0028/0035	F-16C	to Bahrain as 101, 103, 105, 107, 109, 111, 113, 115
90-0036/0039	F-16D	to Bahrain as 150, 152, 154, 156
90-0700/0776	F-16C	
90-0777/0800	F-16D Block 42	'0778 scored first USAF F-16 kill 12/27/92
90-0801/0833	F-16C	
90-0834/0849	F-16D	
90-0850/0874	F-16C	to Israel as 503, 506, 508, 511, 152, 514, 516, 519, 520, 522, 523, 525, 527, 528, 530, 531, 534/536, 538, 539, 542, 543, 546, 547
90-0875/0898	F-16D	to Israel as 601, 603, 606, 610, 612, 615, 619, 621, 624, 628, 630, 633, 637, 638, 642, 647, 648, 651, 652, 656, 660, 664, 666, 667
90-0899/0930	F-16C	to Egypt as 9703/9734

Serial	Version	Notes
90-0931/0937	F-16D	to Egypt as 9601/9607
90-0938/0941	F-16D	to South Korea as 00938/00941
91-0001/0005	F-16C Block 40F	built by TAI for Turkey, *Peace Onyx I*
91-0006/0021	F-16C Block 40J	built by TAI for Turkey, *Peace Onyx I*
91-0022/0024	F-16D Block 40J	built by TAI for Turkey, *Peace Onyx I*
91-0336/0461	F-16C	
91-0462/0485	F-16D	
91-0486/0489	F-16C	
91-0490/0495	F-16D	to Israel as 551, 554, 557, 558
92-0001/0017	F-16C Block 40L	to Israel as 673, 676, 678, 682, 684, 687 built by TAI for Turkey, *Peace Onyx I*
92-0018/0021	F-16C Block 40P	built by TAI for Turkey, *Peace Onyx I*
92-0022/0024	F-16D Block 40L	built by TAI for Turkey, *Peace Onyx I*
92-0100/0218	F-16C	
92-0219/0249	F-16D	
92-3880/3923	F-16C	
92-3924/3927	F-16D	
92-4000/4027	F-16C	
92-4028/4047	F-16D	
93-0001/0014	F-16C Block 40P	built by TAI for Turkey, *Peace Onyx I*
93-0485/0512	F-16C	to Egypt as 9951/9978
93-0513/0524	F-16D	to Egypt as 9851/9862
93-0525/0530	F-16C	to Egypt as 9979/9984
93-0531/0554	F-16C	
93-0657/0690	F-16C Block 40	built by TAI for Turkey as 93-657/690
93-0691/0696	F-16D Block 52	built by TAI for Turkey as 93-691/696
93-0702/0821	F-16A Block 20	to Taiwan as 6601/6720

Serial	Version	Notes
93-0822/0851	F-16B Block 20	to Taiwan as 6801/6830
93-1045/1076	F-16C Block 50D	to Greece as 045/076
93-1077/1084	F-16D Block 50D	to Greece as 077/084
93-4048/4099	F-16C Block 52D	to South Korea
93-4100/4119	F-16D Block 52D	to South Korea
94-0038/0049	F-16C Block 50	
94-0071/0096	F-16C Block 50	built by TAI for Turkey, as 94-071/096
94-0105/0110	F-16D Block 50	built by TAI for Turkey, as 94-105/110
94-0187/0238	F-16C Block 50	
94-0266/0273	F-16C Block 52	to Singapore
94-0274/0283	F-16D Block 52	to Singapore
94-1557/1564	F-16D Block 50	built by TAI for Turkey
96-0080/0085	F-16C/D Block 50	
96-0086/0106	F-16C Block 40	to Egypt, *Peace Vector V*
96-5025/5036	F-16C/D Block 52	
96-5081	F-16C Block 50	
97-0106/0111	F-16C Block 50D	
97-0112/0121	F-16C Block 52	to Singapore
97-0122/0123	F-16D Block 52	to Singapore
98-0003/0005	F-16C Block 50D	
99-0082	F-16C Block 50	
00-0218	F-16CJ	
00-0609	F-16C	
00-6001/6055	F-16C Block 60	for UAE
00-6056/6080	F-16D Block 60	for UAE

Major operators
Belgium

Serial	Version	Notes
78-0116/0161	F-16A	built by SABCA (FA-01/FA-46)
78-0162/0173	F-16B	built by SABCA (FB-01/FB-12)
80-3538/3546	F-16A	built by SABCA (FA-47/55)
80-3547/3587	F-16A Block 15	built by SABCA (FA-56/96)
80-3588/3595	F-16B Block 15	built by SABCA (FB-13/20)
86-0073/0077	F-16A Block 15	built by SABCA (FA-97/101)
87-0001	F-16B Block 15	built by SABCA (FB-21)

Serial	Version	Notes
87-0046/0056	F-16A Block 15	built by SABCA (FA-102/112)
88-0038/0047	F-16A Block 15	built by SABCA (FA-113/122)
88-0048/0049	F-16B Block 15	built by SABCA (FB-22/23)
89-0001/0011	F-16A Block 15	built by SABCA (FA-123/133)
89-0012	F-16B Block 15	built by SABCA (FB-24)
90-0025/0027	F-16A Block 15	built by SABCA (FA-134/136)

Netherlands

Serial	Version	Notes
78-0212/0258	F-16A	built by Fokker (J-212/J-258)
78-0259/0271	F-16B	built by Fokker (J-259/J-271) '0259 (J-259) was first Fokker-built F-16
80-3616/3648	F-16A	built by Fokker (J-316/348)
80-3649/3657	F-16B	built by Fokker (J-649/657)
81-0864/0881	F-16A	built by Fokker (J-864/881)
81-0882	F-16B	built by Fokker (J-882)
81-0884/0885	F-16B	built by Fokker (J-884/J-885)
83-1192/1207	F-16A	built by Fokker (J-192/207)
83-1208/1211	F-16B	built by Fokker (J-208/211)
84-1358/1367	F-16A	built by Fokker (J-358/367)
84-1368/1369	F-16B	built by Fokker (J-368/369)
85-0135/0146	F-16A	built by Fokker (J-135/146)
86-0054/0063	F-16A	built by Fokker (J-054/063)
86-0064/0065	F-16B	built by Fokker (J-064/065)
87-0066/0068	F-16B	built by Fokker (J-066/068)
87-0508/0516	F-16A	built by Fokker (J-508/516)
87-0710	F-16A	to Holland as J-710
88-0001/0012	F-16A	built by Fokker (J-001/J-012)
89-0013/0021	F-16A	built by Fokker (J-013/021) '0021 (J-021) was the last Fokker-built F-16

Israel

Serial	Version	Notes
78-0308/0354	F-16A	
78-0355/0362	F-16B	
80-0649/0668	F-16A	
86-1598/1612	F-16C Block 30	
87-1661/1693	F-16C Block 30	340, 341, 344, 345, 348, 349, 350, 353, 355, 356, 360, 364, 367, 368, 371, 373, 374, 377, 378,381, 384, 386, 388, 389, 391, 393, 394, 392, 397, 388, 383, 385, 379
87-1694/1708	F-16D Block 30	020, 023, 030, 030, 031, 034, 036, 039, 041, 045, 046, 048, 050, 057, 061, 055
88-1709/1711	F-16C Block 30	359, 313, 329
88-1712/1720	F-16D Block 30	065, 069, 070, 072, 074, 077/079, 083
89-0277	F-16C	502
89-0278/0279	F-16C	9701/9702
90-0850/0874	F-16C	503, 506, 508, 511, 152, 514, 516, 519, 520, 522, 523, 525, 527, 528, 530, 531, 534/536, 538, 539, 542, 543, 546, 547
90-0875/0898	F-16D	601, 603, 606, 610, 612, 615, 619, 621, 624, 628, 630, 633, 637, 638, 642, 647, 648, 651, 652, 656, 660, 664, 666, 667
91-0486/0489	F-16C	551, 554, 557, 558
91-0490/0495	F-16D	673, 676, 678, 682, 684, 687

Turkey

Serial	Version	Notes
86-0066/0072	F-16C Block 30B	*Peace Onyx I* first two built by Fort Worth, rest by TAI
86-0191/0196	F-16D	built by Fort Worth
87-0002/0003	F-16D Block 30E	built by TAI, *Peace Onyx I*
87-0009/0018	F-16C Block 30B	built by TAI, *Peace Onyx I*
87-0019/0021	F-16C Block 30E	built by TAI, *Peace Onyx I*
88-0013	F-16D Block 30E	built by TAI, *Peace Onyx I*
88-0014/0015	F-16D Block 40A	built by TAI, *Peace Onyx I*
88-0019/0032	F-16C Block 30E	built by TAI, *Peace Onyx I*
88-0033/0037	F-16C Block 40A	built by TAI, *Peace Onyx I*
89-0022/0033	F-16C Block 40A	built by TAI, *Peace Onyx I*
89-0034/0041	F-16C Block 40D	built by TAI, *Peace Onyx I*
89-0042	F-16D Block 40A	built by TAI, *Peace Onyx I*
89-0043/0045	F-16D Block 40D	built by TAI, *Peace Onyx I*
90-0001/0009	F-16C Block 40D	built by TAI
90-0010/0021	F-16C Block 40F	built by TAI
90-0022/0024	F-16D Block 40F	built by TAI
91-0001/0005	F-16C Block 40F	built by TAI, *Peace Onyx I*
91-0006/0021	F-16C Block 40J	built by TAI, *Peace Onyx I*
91-0022/0024	F-16D Block 40J	built by TAI, *Peace Onyx I*
92-0001/0017	F-16C Block 40L	built by TAI, *Peace Onyx I*
92-0018/0021	F-16C Block 40P	built by TAI, *Peace Onyx I*
92-0022/0024	F-16D Block 40L	built by TAI, *Peace Onyx I*
93-0001/0014	F-16C Block 40P	built by TAI, *Peace Onyx I*

Greece

Serial	Version	Notes
88-0110/0143	F-16C Block 40	110/143
88-0144/0149	F-16D Block 40	144/149
93-1045/1084	F-16D Block 50	045/084

Egypt

Serial	Version	Notes
80-0639/0643	F-16A Block 15	*Peace Vector* (9301/9305)
80-0644/0648	F-16B Block 15	*Peace Vector* (9201/9205)
81-0643/0661	F-16A Block 15	*Peace Vector* (9306/9324)
81-0662	F-16B Block 15	*Peace Vector* 9206
81-0883	F-16B	9207
81-1061	F-16A	
82-1056/1065	F-16A Block 15	*Peace Vector* (9325/9334)
84-1332/1339	F-16C	9501/9508
84-1340/1345	F-16D	9401/9406
85-1518/1543	F-16C	9509-9534
90-0899/0930	F-16C	9703/9734
90-0931/0937	F-16D	9601/9607
93-0485/0512	F-16C	9951/9978
93-0513/0524	F-16D	9851/9862
93-0525/0530	F-16C	9979/9984

Pakistan

Serial	Version	Notes
81-0899/0930	F-16A	701/728 '0927/'0930 were cancelled
81-0931/0938	F-16B	601/608
81-1504/1507	F-16B	609/612
90-0942/0947	F-16A	729/734
90-0948/0952	F-16B	613/617
92-0404/0451	F-16A	ordered as 92735/92782 '0404/'0410 embargoed at AMARC, rest cancelled
92-0452/0463	F-16B	ordered as 91618/91629 '0452/'0455 embargoed at AMARC, rest cancelled

Denmark

Serial	Version	Notes
78-0174/0203	F-16A Block 1	built by SABCA (E-174/E-203)
78-0204/0211	F-16B Block 1	built by SABCA (ET-204/ET-211)
80-3596/3611	F-16A Block 1	built by SABCA (E-596/611)

Serial	Version	Notes
80-3612/3615	F-16B Block 1	built by SABCA (ET-612/615)
86-0197/0199	F-16B Block 15	built by Fokker (ET-197/199)
87-0004/0008	F-16A Block 15	built by Fokker (E-004/008)
87-0022	F-16B Block 15	built by Fokker (ET-022)
88-0016/0018	F-16A Block 15	built by Fokker (E-016/018)

Norway

Serial	Version	Notes
78-0272/0300	F-16A	built by Fokker (272/300)
78-0301/0307	F-16B	built by Fokker (301/307)
80-3658/3688	F-16A	built by Fokker (658/688)
80-3689/3693	F-16B	built by Fokker (689/693)
87-0711/0712	F-16B	to Norway as 711/712

Portugal

Serial	Version	Notes
93-0465/0481	F-16A	16101/16117
93-0482/0484	F-16B	16118/16120

South Korea

Serial	Version	Notes
84-1370/1373	F-16D	41370/41373
85-1384/1385	F-16D	
85-1574/1583	F-16C	51574/51583
85-1584/1585	F-16D	51584/51585
86-1586/1597	F-16C	
87-1653/1660	F-16C	71653/71660
90-0938/0941	F-16D	00938/00941
92-4000	F-16C Block 52G	92-000
92-4001	F-16C Block 52H	92-001
92-4002/4003	F-16C Block 52J	92-002/003
92-4004/4008	F-16C Block 52K	92-004/008
92-4009/4013	F-16C Block 52L	92-009/013
92-4014/4017	F-16C Block 52M	92-014/017
92-4018/4027	F-16C Block 52N	92-018/027
92-4028/4031	F-16D Block 52G	92-028/031
92-4032/4037	F-16D Block 52H	92-032/037
92-4038	F-16D Block 52K	92-038
92-4039	F-16D Block 52L	92-039
92-4040/4041	F-16D Block 52M	92-040/041
92-4042/4047	F-16D Block 52N	92-042/047
93-4048/4099	F-16C Block 52D	
93-4100/4119	F-16D Block 52D	

Appendix 3. Museum Aircraft

USA

Not surprisingly the United States has the greater majority of Fighting Falcon exhibits. Most are from the earliest batches of pre-production and production machines, although there are some 'specials' on display. Possibly indicative of their permanent grounding, at least five ex-US Navy machines are now on display. It is highly unlikely that any preserved F-16s will fly in private hands, since support of such a complicated aircraft is beyond the resources of private individuals and organisations.

Version	Serial	Location
F-16N	163269	San Diego Aerospace Museum (CA)
F-16N	163271	Pacific Coast (CA) Air Museum (Formerly USAF 85-01372)
F-16N	163277	Palm Springs Aviation Museum (CA)
F-16N	163569	Fort Worth NAS (TX)
F-16N	163572	Pensacola NAS (FL) Displayed outdoors
YF-16	72-01567	Hampton (VA), Air and Space Museum
F-16A	75-00745	Wright Patterson AFB Museum (OH) as '79-317'
F-16A FSD	75-00748	Colorado Springs (CO), USAF Academy
F-16A	75-00750	Wright Patterson AFB Museum (OH), AFTI test-bed
F-16A FSD	75-00751	Edwards AFB (CA)
F-16B	75-00752	Frontiers of Flight Museum, Dallas (TX)
F-16	78-00001	Langley AFB (VA)
F-16A	78-00005	Tuscon IAP, (AZ) AZ ANG
F-16A	78-00025	Nellis AFB (NV)
F-16A	78-00042	Alabama ANG, Montgomery (AL)
F-16A	78-00052	Eielson AFB (AK)
F-16A	78-00053	Misawa AB (Japan)
F-16A	78-00057	Spangdahlem AB (Germany)
F-16A	78-00059	Selfridge ANGB (MI) Museum
F-16A	78-00061	Alabama ANG, Montgomery (AL)
F-16B	78-00107	Lackland AFB (TX) Parade ground

Version	Serial	Location
F-16B	79-00101	Space Museum, Huntsville (AL)
F-16A	79-0373	Buckley ANGB (CO)
F-16A	79-00388	Hill AFB (UT) Museum as '388FW'
F-16A	79-00403	New York (NY), USS Intrepid aircraft carrier
F-16A	80-00573	Eglin AFB (FL) Museum
F-16A	82-00390	Ellington Field, ANG Base, (TX)

Belgium

The airframes on display in Belgium are from the earliest part of the production run and have been withdrawn from use for numerous reasons, the main of which is a lack of upgradability. A large, fluid quantity of machines is stored at Weelde AB. These aircraft are being held as part of the strategic reserve, for spares recovery and as a means of levelling out the flying hours and fatigue index across the fleet.

Version	Serial	Location
F-16A	FA-01	Brussels Museum Pacific Coast
F-16A	FA-04	Florennes
F-16A	FA-03	Saffraanberg Instructional
F-16A	FA-10	Bevekom/ Beauvechain
F-16B	FB-03	Saffraanberg Instructional

Italy

As Aviano AB has increased in importance owing to operations over the Balkans, so the need for an instructional airframe became apparent. Thus, the retired F-16A 79-0340 was despatched to fulfil this need.

Version	Serial	Location
F-16A	79-0340	Aviano Display/ Instructional

Netherlands

The Netherlands uses its redundant Fighting

Falcons for display and instructional purposes. Many of these airframes are life expired and will not fly again.

Version	Serial	Location
F-16A	J-015	Schaarsbergen Display/ Instructional
F-16A	J-219	Leeuwarden Display/ Instructional
F-16A	J-238	Schaarsbergen Display/ Instructional
F-16A	J-245	Leeuwarden Display/ Instructional
F-16A	J-247	Twenthe Display/ Instructional
F-16B	J-260	Woensdrecht Display
F-16B	J-263	Schaarsbergen Display/ Instructional

Norway

Norway has such a small fleet of F-16s that its only display/instructional airframe is an ex-USAF machine delivered courtesy of AMARC.

Version	Serial	Location
F-16A	81-0683	Kjevik Instructional/ Display ex-USAF machine

Although the number of preserved and withdrawn F-16s is currently small, their number will increase as time passes and older machines are withdrawn.

The first production F-16A, FA-01 for the Belgian air force, has been interred in the Koninklijk Leger Museum, Brussels since July 1997. *(Eric Dewhurst)*

Appendix 4. Model Kits

Even as General Dynamics was rolling the first YF-16 prototype out onto the concrete at Fort Worth, the model aircraft kit manufacturers were investing in the necessary hardware to manufacture kits of the new fighter. First off the blocks was the American manufacturer Revell Inc, which released its YF-16 not long after the real machine had appeared. Since that date various manufacturers have added the type to their ranges in a selection of scales. In addition, a veritable plethora of after-market specialists produces a full range of decals, conversions and add on detail packs. In fact there is no excuse for any modeller not to add an F-16 to their display, with virtually all variations being covered. Listed below are the kits currently available.

Academy

Aircraft	Scale
YF-16A Falcon	1:72
F-16C Fighting Falcon	1:48
F-16C Thunderbirds	1:48

Airfix

Aircraft	Scale
F-16A/B Fighting Falcon	1:72
F-16XL	1:144

AMT/Ertl

Aircraft	Scale
F-16A Thunderbird Flight set	1:72

Hasegawa

Aircraft	Scale
F-16C Fighting Falcon	1:48
F-16B Plus Fighting Falcon	1:48
F-16D Fighting Falcon	1:48
F-16C Night Falcon	1:48
F-16CJ (Block 50) Fighting Falcon	1:48
F-16C 35 FW Misawa Japan	1:48
F-16B Plus Fighting Falcon	1:72
F-16DJ (Block 50) Fighting Falcon	1:72
F-16CG (Block 40) Fighting Falcon	1:72
F-16A Black Knights RSAF	1:72
F-16A Plus Fighting Falcon	1:72
YF-16CCV	1:72
F-16C Fighting Falcon	1:72
F-16N Top Gun	1:72
F-16D Thunderbirds	1:72
F-16D Falcon Vista	1:72
F-16B	1:72
F-16D	1:72
F-16CJ Block 50 Fighting Falcon	1:72
F-16C Wisconsin ANG	1:72
F-16CJ 79th Anniversary	1:48
F-16A USAF/Dutch/ Danish	1:32

Hasegawa (continued)

Aircraft	Scale
F-16C Fighting Falcon USAFE	1:32
F-16C Fighting Falcon	1:72
F-16C 'Blue Nose'	1:48
F-16D Thunderbirds	1:48
F-16CJ Weapons School Taxi cab	1:48
F-16A Black Knights RSAF	1:48

Italeri

Aircraft	Scale
F-16 Cockpit	1:16
F-16A/B Fighting Falcon	1:72
F-16C/D Night Falcon	1:72
F-16C/D	1:48
F-16A NATO Fighter	1:48
F-16B/D 'Viper'	1:48
F-16A/B NATO Falcon	1:72

Kangnam Models

Aircraft	Scale
F-16	1:32
F-16XL	1:32

Matchbox

Aircraft	Scale
F-16B Royal Netherlands Air Force	1:72

Minicraft

Aircraft	Scale
F-16A Falcon	1:144

PM

Aircraft	Scale
Turkish F-16	1:72

Revell

Aircraft	Scale
GD F-16A Fighting Falcon	1:144
F-16C	1:144
F-16A KLU 313 Sqn Display 1994	1:72

Revell (continued)

Aircraft	Scale
F-16C Falcon	1:48
F-16A KLU Tigermeet 1991 RNAF	1:72
GD F-16A Fighting Falcon	1:72
F-16A Tigermeet	1:48
F-16A MLU Belgium and Dutch	1:72
F-16C Block 50/52 USAF	1:72

Smer

Aircraft	Scale
F-16A Fighting Falcon	1:72

Tamiya

Aircraft	Scale
YF-16	1:48

Appendix 5. Further Reading

F-16 Fighting Falcon by Robbie Shaw, Motorbooks International, February 1996

Basher Five-Two: The True Story of F-16 Fighter Pilot Captain Scott O'Grady by Scott O'Grady, Bantam Books, June 1997

Arms Deal: The Selling of the F-Sixteen by Ingemar Dorfer, Praeger Pub Text, February 1983

Viper F-16 (Modern Military Aircraft) by Lou Drendel, Squadron/Signal Publications, December 1992

F-16A and B Fighting Falcon: In Detail & Scale by Bert Kinzey, Aero Pub., June 1982

F-16 Fighting Falcon by Bill Gunston, Motorbooks International, June 1983

F-16 Fighting Falcon in Action by Lou Drendel, Squadron/Signal Publications, August 1983

F-16 Fighting Falcons (Osprey Military Aircraft) by David F. Brown and Robert F. Dorr, Osprey Publishing, September 1992

General Dynamics F-16 by William G. Holder, Aero Publishers

General Dynamics F-16 Fighting Falcon (With Record) by Jay Miller, Aviation Book Co, August 1982

General Dynamics F-16 by William G. Holder, Aero Pub, November 1983

Modern Fighting Aircraft F-16 Fighting Falcon, Volume 2 by Douglas Richardson, Arco Pub, October 1983

Walk around F-16 Fighting Falcon by Lou Drendel, Squadron/Signal Publications

F-16 Fighting Falcon, Crescent Books, March 1992

F-16 Fighting Falcon by Peter R. Foster, Motorbooks International (Short Disc), June 1989

F-16 Fighting Falcon (Aero Series, Vol. 42) by Bill Siuru and Bill Holder, Aero Pub, May 1991

F-16 Fighting Falcon (Combat Aircraft Series) by Doug Richardson, Crescent Books, March 1992

General Dynamics F-16 Fighting Falcon (Classic Warplanes) by Doug Richardson, Gallery Books, March 1990

Le F-16: vedette de l'aviation americaine (In French) by Jean-Luc Beghin and Pierre Sparaco, Dupuis, 1978

F-16 Fighting Falcon by Tim Senior, Key Publishing, 2002

Combat Legend Boeing F-15 Eagle and Strike Eagle by Steve Davies, Airlife Publishing Ltd, 2002

Index